The Resilient Healthcare Organization

The Resilient Healthcare Organization

How to Reduce Physician and Healthcare Worker Burnout

George Mayzell, MD, MBA

LONDON AND NEW YORK

First published 2020 by Routledge

2 Park Square, Milton Park, Abingdon, Oxon OX14 4RN
605 Third Avenue, New York, NY 10017

Routledge is an imprint of the Taylor & rancis Group, an informa business

First issued in paperback 2021

Publisher's Note

The publisher has gone to great lengths to ensure the quality of this reprint but points out that some imperfections in the original copies may be apparent.

ISBN-13: 978-0-367-24993-9 (hbk)
ISBN-13: 978-1-03-217302-3 (pbk)
DOI: 10.4324/9780429286025

Library of Congress Cataloging-in-Publication Data

Names: Mayzell, George, author.
Title: The resilient healthcare organization : how to reduce physician and healthcare worker burnout / George Mayzell.
Description: New York, NY : Routledge, 2020. | Includes bibliographical references and index.
Identifiers: LCCN 2019050427 (print) | LCCN 2019050428 (ebook) | ISBN 9780367249939 (hardback) (alk. paper) | ISBN 9780429286025 (ebook)
Subjects: MESH: Burnout, Professional--prevention & control | Health Personnel--psychology
Classification: LCC R690 (print) | LCC R690 (ebook) | NLM WA 495 | DDC 158.7/23--dc23
LC record available at https://lccn.loc.gov/2019050427
LC ebook record available at https://lccn.loc.gov/2019050428

Visit the Taylor & Francis Web site at
http://www.taylorandfrancis.com

and the CRC Press Web site at
http://www.crcpress.com

Contents

Acknowledgement

A special thank you to Dr. Dan Edelman for his contributions to this book and especially his thought provoking insights and discussions on the electronic medical record.

About the Author

George Mayzell, MD, MBA, FACHE, is the founder and president of Empowered Healthcare, which specializes in population health, care management redesign, clinical variation, clinical integration, and physician leadership. He was the past chief clinical officer of Vizient Southeast.

Prior to that he was the senior vice president/chief medical officer and chief clinical integration officer for AMITA Health, an integrated health system serving communities in western and northwestern suburban Chicago. AMITA Health is a Joint Operating Company formed in February 2015 by Adventist Midwest Health and Alexian Brothers Health System, encompassing nine hospitals and an extensive physician provider network of more than 3,000 physicians.

Dr. Mayzell joined Adventist Midwest Health in January 2013, after serving as CEO of Health Choice (a PHO and CIN) and senior vice president of Methodist Le Bonheur Healthcare in Memphis, Tennessee.

He previously served as senior medical director of managed care for University of Florida and Shands Hospital. He spent more than ten years with Blue Cross Blue Shield of Florida, working as regional medical director for care and quality and corporate managing medical director for pharmacy and care. Additionally, he has more than ten years of practice experience.

Dr. Mayzell is a board-certified internist and geriatrician. He received his medical degree from the Rutgers University, New Jersey, and his MBA from Jacksonville University, Florida.

Dr. Mayzell has co-authored several books including *Leveraging Lean in Healthcare* and *Physician Alignment*, as well as *Population Health*.

Contributor Bios

Kathleen Ferket, MSN, APN-BC, is an experienced and transformational nursing executive, speaker, author, and a recognized leader in case management, clinical integration, value-based care, and population health.

Kathy consults with organizations across the care continuum to achieve value-based care outcomes and is currently a senior consultant with the American Case Management Association.

Most recently, she served as Care Continuum Vice President for a nine-hospital system in the Midwest where she led acute care management and alignment for post-acute services for the health system. Previous executive roles included hospital operations, service line leadership, clinical reliability, and population health initiatives.

As a board-certified nurse practitioner, Kathy has been recognized by the Nursing Spectrum for Advancing Nursing Practice and received the Ron Lee Lifetime Achievement award from the Illinois Department of Public Health. Kathy volunteers for the Illinois Multiple Sclerosis Foundation and has served on the Board of Directors for the Illinois Organization of Nurse Leaders and the Infant Welfare Society. As a registered leadership coach and Green Belt LEAN champion, Kathy mentors leaders in navigating change, workplace conflict, teambuilding, and purposeful communication. She has published in peer-reviewed nursing journals and contributed to book chapters on Patient Safety and Population Health. Kathy received her Bachelor's in Nursing degree from DePaul University and a Master of Nursing degree from Rush University.

Bruce Flareau, MD, FAAFP, CPE, FACPE, is a highly experienced senior physician executive, multi book author, executive coach, and national speaker on topics ranging from physician leadership, population health, and care transformation. He has a proven track record of organizational effectiveness and extensive experience in governance, strategic planning, change management and operational execution in large health systems.

Dr. Flareau has held numerous leadership roles including chief medical informatics officer, founding president of one of the best performing Clinically Integrated Networks and ACOs in the United States, and EVP Chief Medical Officer of a large top performing health system in the Southeast.

Dr. Flareau has been recognized as a full professor at two universities and was a founding residency program director. He obtained his medical degree from State University of New York, Upstate Medical Center, Syracuse, and completed his family medicine residency at Bayfront Medical Center in Florida. He is a certified physician executive and a fellow of the American Academy of Family Physicians and the American College of Physician Executives.

Patricia S. Normand, MD, is an associate professor in the Departments of Psychiatry and Preventive Medicine at Rush University Medical Center and is the Director of Wellness and Integrative Health, RUMC Road Home: The Center for Veterans and Their Families and the Director of the Mindfulness Based Stress Reduction program at RUMC. After completing residency and a fellowship in psychiatry at Massachusetts General Hospital she remained on faculty at Harvard Medical School and on staff at MGH in the Psychiatric Outpatient Consultation-Liaison Program. She consults on wellness and burnout prevention, as well as mindfulness and integrative health programs in a variety of settings.

Introduction

Awareness regarding healthcare workforce stress, depression, burnout, and suicidality has finally come to the forefront in our industry. Finally … and it's about darn time!

For far too many years, those in the workforce who are now in the later stages of their careers often recognized that becoming "burnt-out" was an inherent risk to their profession. Being more resilient was not even a term utilized until more recent times. "Sucking-it-up" and just dealing with the stress burden was the expectation. And it was well appreciated that some individuals just somehow seemed to do better at it than others, while a few casualties, unfortunately, also occurred along the way.

But speaking up on the causation for those casualties was never considered, and moving beyond a vague under-the-radar awareness of the expected need to just be tough was rarely considered or even mentioned in conversations.

However, at our most simple core, we all want to feel safe, be healthy, stay happy, and be able to live our lives with ease and minimal discomfort. The manner in which we individually choose to pursue our personal and professional satisfaction heavily factors into how successful we become in meeting these four core needs over the course of our lives. Healthcare's frontline workforce is well recognized to be strongly altruistic and highly committed to providing care for others, but it is always under duress nowadays and increasingly requires closer consideration for how to maintain its own wellness. Fortunately, this recognition has now come out of the shadows and into the forefront of our industry's awareness.

The strongly altruistic and compassionate healthcare workforce clearly needs much more attention to the genesis and maintenance of its own well-being and health.

The global industry of healthcare is inherently complex, and the degree of complexity continues to escalate with an increasingly rapid momentum. The variety of different sectors in the industry collectively helps create a whirlwind of influences that contribute to this complexity, while, simultaneously, the host and variety of healthcare delivery systems are continuously seeking solutions to better manage the whirlwind's trickle-down effects. Additionally, in attempting to refine their own approaches toward true patient-centered care that embraces shared decision-making at all levels, physicians and other healthcare workforce providers are far too often entrapped in this intricate, but externally generated, web of competing values and influences – most of which may be poorly realized or understood by the providers.

Increased productivity pressures, encroachment of the electronic health record, decreasing reimbursements for care, escalating turnover with subsequent increased workloads for others, and a residual debt load from training are just a few of the stressors resulting from the complexity of healthcare today and experienced by the current healthcare workforce. Their negative aspects and impact on the workforce are staggering. While the data is still accruing and the initial reports regarding depression and burnout rates are uncomfortable to absorb, one of the most disheartening facts is that more than one physician per day commits suicide (400 per year) – rates two to three times higher than the general population on a per capita basis.

While there is no doubt that there are a few example patient care delivery environments slowly undergoing change as they try to expedite an improved quality of life for their healthcare workforces, there is still much more needed to be accomplished before any statements can be made that the industry is successfully and consistently looking after its workforce environments properly.

The title of this book – *The Resilient Healthcare Organization* – provides an initial hint of its content and its purpose. The actual substance of the book, fortunately, delivers far more than providing simple hints and peripherally relevant suggestions regarding an extremely sensitive topic area in healthcare. The book's approach nicely details the issues and concerns around the topic and is then structured to provide tangible approaches at the individual and organizational levels for how to better address the issues related to burnout. It is incumbent for all healthcare delivery systems to begin tackling these issues at the organizational levels. But it is also incumbent for individual providers (physicians, nurses, pharmacists, allied healthcare providers, etc.) to re-learn how to approach remaining healthy and well as they progress through their careers. This book definitely helps both organizations and individuals with how to refine the inadequate current approaches to a happier, healthier, and more satisfied workforce.

Unfortunately, our healthcare education institutions have not yet begun to effectively address these issues proactively as yet. Trainees of all types are still not adequately prepared on how to manage their expectations for functioning effectively with their behaviors, emotions, and mental health once they actually enter the workforce. Graduating trainees are already demonstrating resilience for having completed their education tracks, but they then need to re-learn new approaches for resiliency as they engage in their career paths. Our education systems still need to do better in this regard. And less we forget, there are significant concerns for burnout in the trainee populations as well.

The association I am privileged to lead – the American Association for Physician Leadership – maximizes the potential of physician leadership to create significant personal and organizational transformation. In this role, I routinely encourage each of us in healthcare (not just physicians) to continue seeking deeper levels of satisfaction in our professional development – and to appreciate better how we can each generate positive influence at all levels. As physician leaders (since each of us is one), I also urge all of us to get more engaged, stay engaged, and help others in the industry's workforce to become further engaged with creating a broader level of positive change in healthcare. A healthier workforce is essential for improved patient care and the ongoing evolution of a better healthcare delivery system overall.

The Resilient Healthcare Organization is an enjoyable read with a pragmatic value for all those attempting to create change in healthcare. Relish the book's read and your learnings of the opportunities outlined within its pages. Most importantly, continue to pursue your own life where you are able to feel safe, be healthy, stay happy, and able to live with ease and minimal discomfort. Your career choices and how you continue to help others truly make a difference!

Peter B. Angood, MD, FRCS(C), FACS, MCCM, FAAPL (Hon)
President & CEO
American Association for Physician Leadership
Washington D.C.

Chapter 1

How We Got Here

George Mayzell

Contents

Overview

It has always been difficult and challenging to be a healthcare provider. The competition to get into medical or nursing school sets the stage for many sleepless nights and stressful encounters. There is a built-in selection process as well as "on-the-job training" to prepare for a difficult, challenging, but potentially rewarding career. This is what was typically expected when one first decided to venture into a healthcare career. There is a certain personal resiliency required to endure the training process, such as the endless studying, late nights, and difficult patient interactions that prepare the provider to be flexible and tough enough to deal with difficult and challenging encounters, often without sleep.

When you talk to healthcare providers today, most of them feel like they got more than they bargained for when they started on their journeys. No one could have expected the additional administrative burdens and administrative oversight obligations that are now part of everyday medicine. In addition to these challenges, the electronic medical record has arguably not made it easier to deliver healthcare. The merits and advantages can certainly be argued and debated, but few healthcare professionals feel like it has made their job easier or more efficient. And finally, the new business pressures of healthcare economics have driven most physicians into new employment models, which can be challenging and in many cases different from their original career expectations.

ALL of the above have contributed to the increasing stress and pressures of practicing medicine in today's environment. This has led to a growing concern about physician burnout.

Recently there's been much debate over the term "burnout." The consensus is that burnout has a negative connotation and seems to suggest that it is a personal failing – that the person could not endure the stresses and pressures of their work environment. Several new terms have been introduced, including terms such as "moral injury," and other similar terms.[1] We like the term "disillusionment" since there really seems to be a disconnect between expectations and the new reality. The frustration seems to come from the difficulties in working through all of the non-patient care issues that get in the way of patient care.

What is interesting about burnout is that, if we look back 15 or 20 years, we do not see or recognize the degree of burnout that we see today. Certainly some of it was there, but arguably not anywhere near what we see today. Were physicians working fewer hours? Was there less work/life balance? I don't think so. Here we postulate that it really is not about the additional work or the additional hours physicians and healthcare workers may be putting in, but more about new stresses, such as the lack of control, lack of respect, administrative burdens, and lack of patient engagement/relationship, that are different today. With this in mind, we have to focus on "what is different" today so that we can mitigate some of these changes.

The term "burnout" was initially coined by Herbert Freudenberger, an American psychologist back in the 1970s. He described the syndrome as "becoming exhausted by making excessive demands on energy, strength, or resources" in the workplace.[2] While this term is used in the press, perhaps it is not really descriptive. What we are really experiencing is physician and healthcare worker "disillusionment."

Disillusionment is a misalignment of expectations and autonomy with the current healthcare system. This includes the introduction of new employment models, new patient models, and the use of advanced practice professionals including hospitalists, intensivists, and others. All of these things have fragmented healthcare in ways that could not have been fully anticipated and have affected negatively the experience of the healthcare worker.

All of these pressures and unexpected administrative burdens have made many healthcare providers less than happy with their choice of profession. These changes in pressures, while leading to some dissatisfaction, have to be differentiated from burnout. Whereas the day-to-day stresses of healthcare can sometimes be an adaptive response to external pressures and force an individual to focus on working harder and faster, burnout is much the opposite. Some of the main definers of burnout are physical exhaustion and apathy.[3–5] Obviously, this is not productive.

Each year it is estimated that between 300 and 400 doctors commit suicide. This is a physician suicide rate of between 28 and 40 per 100,000, much higher than public suicide rates. Most people believe this number is grossly underestimated. Physician suicide has been documented and noted to be a problem since the 1920s. This suicide rate must be contrasted with the general population's suicide rate of 12.3 per 100,000. This is a topic that is not generally discussed publicly and may be partially related to depression and substance abuse issues[6, 7] (Figure 1.1).

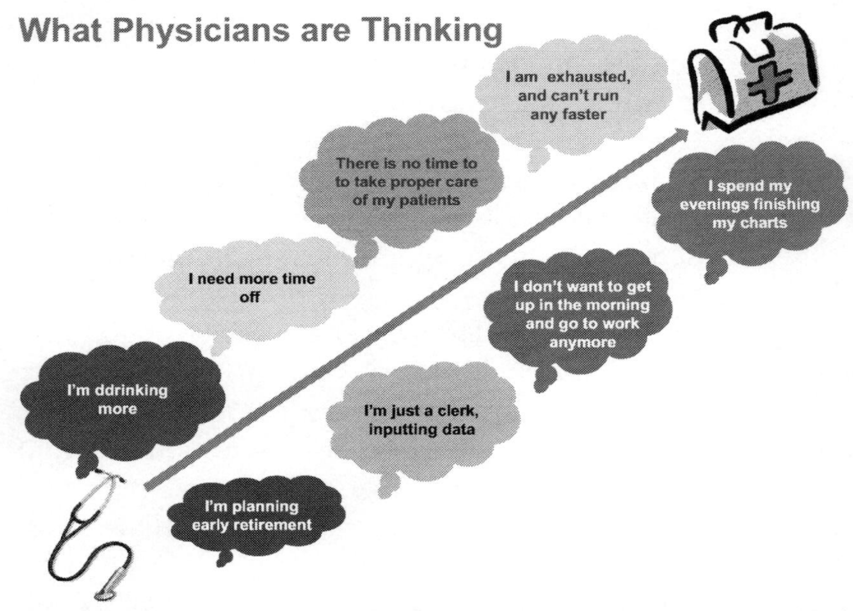

Figure 1.1 What physicians are thinking and saying

The stigma of depression, mental illness, substance abuse, and suicide in physicians is far more significant than in the lay public. People's faith and confidence in their role as patients are at risk. The stoic rigor of the training teaches physicians to ignore and not seek help for these very real issues.

There is also the very practical issue of medical licensure and the risk of losing continued livelihood. Applying for staff privileges at hospitals, payers, and licensure can be at risk if mental health or substance abuse issues are disclosed.

With this in mind, how do we augment the resiliency that was part of the selection process and training process to become a healthcare clinician? How do we use it to focus energy to ultimately improve care for the patient and well-being for the provider?

Resiliency has been defined by the American Psychological Association as "the process of adapting well in the face of adversity, trauma, tragedy, threats, or significant sources of stress."[8] Sometimes that is how healthcare providers feel, like they have been bent, compressed, and stretched. This resiliency gets us to the new normal, and one hopes it will prevent the catastrophic symptoms of burnout. On the opposite side of the spectrum of burnout is physician and nursing engagement. This is the anti-burnout. Resiliency is the stretchy piece between burnout and engagement that keeps pulling us back to the center and hopefully keeps us grounded.

One of the more challenging issues is that we are still defining the term "burnout." I think at this point it is generally understood what it is, but the true prevalence and effects are still being sorted through. When investigators looked at the different studies measuring physician burnout, they found much heterogeneity, making it too difficult to categorize consistent themes. The prevalence rates were so varied, including a range of 0% to 80.5%.[9] This makes it very difficult to assess the true prevalence. Is this a true dichotomy, that is, you have or do not have burnout, or is it a continuous variable with degrees of burnout that can be categorized? There is also a strong overlap between burnout and major depression, which needs to be explored further.[8]

To the world outside of healthcare, it may be hard to understand why healthcare workers burn out. They understand some of the emotional stresses of being a healthcare provider, but they don't understand the added pressures. They see someone who has dedicated five to ten or more years to education, someone who is above average in intelligence, has a large house with two cars, and sends the kids to private school. They know that there is respect for this person in the community. So what is all this complaining about? (Figure 1.2).

What they don't understand is that healthcare workers, and physicians in particular, were not trained for the new complexities of healthcare, including team-based care, leadership responsibilities, new employment structures, and a new political environment. It is no longer just about taking care of your patient; it is about working your way through the system to make sure patients get good care, all the while charting it in a

Sources of Burnout

1. Work overload
2. Lack of control
3. Insufficient reward
4. Unfairness
5. Breakdown of community
6. Value conflict

Maslach & Leiter, 1997. "The Truth About Burnout: How Organizations Cause Personal Stress and What to Do About It."

Figure 1.2 What are the sources of burnout?

non-user-friendly electronic medical record and dealing with a litigious society.

We are now exploring different tools to assess burnout and trying to simplify what is clearly something that does not lend itself to simplification. While we might know what it is when we see it, we still do not really have a good handle on the entire burnout continuum.

Christina Maslach herself, the developer of the Maslach Burnout Inventory (MBI), defined burnout as "an erosion of the soul caused by a deterioration of one's values, dignity, spirit, and will."[10] This seems to be even more true in today's healthcare.

It is important not to confuse stress with burnout. Stress can be an adaptive mechanism in which the body's response to a difficult situation elicits one's flight-or-fight response, pushing the body forward. Stress is a temporary emotion, and when we are taken away from the stressor, the body recovers and functions normally before being stressed again (Figure 1.3).

One expects being a physician or a healthcare worker to be stressful, and this is backed by the training process. What is new is the administrative stressors that become part

Stress vs. Burnout	
Stress	**Burnout**
Characterized by overengagement	Characterized by disengagement
Emotions are overreactive	Emotions are blunted
Produces urgency and hyperactivity	Produces helplessness and hopelessness
Loss of energy	Loss of motivation, ideals, and hope
Leads to anxiety disorders	Leads to detachment and depression
Primary damage is physical	Primary damage is emotional
May kill you prematurely	May make life seem not worth living

Figure 1.3 Is a stress or burnout? Source: Adapted from https://keydifferences.com/difference-between-stress-and-burnout.html[11]; https://www.15minutes4me.com/difference-stress/[12]; https://academic.oup.com/bjaed/article/17/10/334/3865410[13]

of physicians' and nurses' everyday routines. They are not trained or adapted for these new experiences. The increasing pressure of work/life balance, a 24-hour information cycle, the smart phone, social media, and instant communications only increase the stress in our work and nonwork environment.

Additionally, recent events have come to light that have prompted healthcare workers to officially recognize burnout as a term or a syndrome. There are now eight official diagnosable conditions under the term "burnout," according to the World Health Organization (WHO). It has yet to make it into the *DSM*. One of the challenges, even though burnout is now diagnosable, is that the diagnosis terms are still very qualitative rather than quantitative.[14] This will be discussed in later chapters.

In this book, we hope to take a less traditional approach to dealing with healthcare worker burnout and resiliency. My contention is that the etiology of burnout is more about the changes in healthcare, aligning values and expectations, and aligning physician and patient values. I hope to focus more on some of the systemic and societal solutions that can help mitigate this very real issue that has the potential to have a direct impact on our healthcare delivery model over the foreseeable future.

Bibliography

1. Cheney, C. (2019, March 25). Are your physicians suffering from burnout – Or moral injury? Retrieved from https://www.healthleadersmedia.com/clinical-care/are-your-physicians-suffering-burnout-or-moral-injury.
2. Heinemann, L.V., & Heinemann, T. (2017, March 6) . Burnout research: Emergence and scientific investigation of a contested diagnosis. *SAGE Open*, 7 (1), 1–12.
3. Drummond, D. (2014). *Stop Physician Burnout: What to Do When Working Harder Isn't Working*. Heritage Press Publications, LLC.
4. Khatri, B.O. (2018). *Healthcare 911: How America's Broken Healthcare System Is Driving Doctors to Despair, Depriving Patients of Care, and Destroying Our Reputation in the World.* Milwaukee, WI: Hansa House Publishing, LLC (in collaboration with HenschelHAUS Publishing, Inc.)
5. Maslach, C., Schaufeli, W.B., & Leiter, M.P. (2001). Job burnout. *Annual Review of Psychology, 52*, 397–422.
6. Castellucci, M. (2018, September 29). Healthcare industry takes on high physician suicide rates, mental health stigma. Retrieved from http://www.modernhealthcare.com/article/20180929/NEWS/180929901.
7. Anderson, P. (2018, May 8). Doctors' suicide rate highest of any profession. Retrieved from https://www.webmd.com/mental-health/news/20180508/doctors-suicide-rate-highest-of-any-profession.
8. The road to resilience, American Psychological Association members publication. Retrieved from HT to//WW W.APA.org/help center/road- Resilience.
9. Schwenk, T.L., & Gold, K.J. (2018, September 18). Physician burnout – A serious symptom, but of what? *JAMA: The Journal of the American Medical Association, 320*(11), 1109–1110.

10. Drummond, D. (blog post, n.d.). Physician burnout: Why it's not a fair fight. Retrieved from https://www.thehappymd.com/blog/bid/295048/physician-burnout-why-its-not-a-fair-fight.
11. Surbhi, S. (2017, November 11). Difference between stress and burnout. Retrieved from https://keydifferences.com/difference-between-stress-and-burnout.html.
12. Differences between stress and burnout? – 15 minutes 4 me. Retrieved from https://www.15minutes4me.com/difference-stress/.
13. Wong, Adrian View-Kim, & Olusegun, Olusanya (2017, October). Burnout and resilience in anesthesia and intensive care medicine. *BJA Education*, *17*(10), 334–340. Retrieved from https://academic.oup.com/bjaed/article/17/10/334/3865410.
14. Borysenko (2019, May 29). Karlyn burnout is now an officially diagnosable condition; here's what you need to know about it. *Forbes*.
15. Cheney, C. (2019, February 22). Physician burnout rate drops 10.5 points after spike. Retrieved from https://www.healthleadersmedia.com/clinical-care/physician-burnout-rate-drops-105-points-after-spike.
16. El-Aswad, N., Ghossoub, Z., & Nadler, R. (2017). *Physician Burnout: An Emotionally Malignant Disease*. North Charleston, SC: CreateSpace Independent Publishing Platform.
17. Wolf, M., & Gillis, S. (2017). *The Other Side of Burnout: Solutions for Healthcare Professionals*. Indianapolis, IN: Dog Ear Publishing.
18. Comas-Diaz, L., Luthar, S.S., Maddi, S.R., O'Neill, H.K., Saakvitne, K., Tedeschi, R. (2014). The road to resilience. *American Psychological Association*. Retrieved from https://www.apa.org/helpcenter/road-resilience.

Chapter 2

What Is Burnout: "The Disillusioned Physician Syndrome"

George Mayzell

Contents

Burnout has three separate aspects. These include a sense of emotional exhaustion, increasing cynicism and depersonalization, and a sense of low personal accomplishment, which leads to a feeling of decreased effectiveness at work.[1, 2] In fact, you must have some combination of all of these three items in order to meet the definition of burnout. Unfortunately, one of the challenges is that there is no commonly agreed-upon, objective definition of burnout. This makes it very difficult to compare studies and accurately identify individuals consistently across the healthcare continuum. Burnout has been around a long time; however, it is only recently that it has been brought to the forefront.

DEFINITIONS

1. Syndrome of emotional exhaustion, depersonalization, and a sense of low personal accomplishment that leads to decreased effectiveness at work.[3]
2. A long-term stress reaction marked by emotional exhaustion, depersonalization, and a lack of sense of personal accomplishment.[3]

The prevalence of burnout seems to be increasing, with rates going up from 45.8% in 2011 to 54.5% in 2014. It is alarming that this syndrome is present (at least in some degree) in over 50% of physicians, but also in advanced practice providers, nurses, and other clinical staff.[4.] Of course, this kind of data is exceptionally challenging since there is no consistent objective definition of burnout. Without this kind of consistency, any numbers that are published are hard to compare. What is clear, however ,is that this is a significant issue for physician and healthcare providers and must be dealt with urgently.

Recently an article from health leaders noted an actual drop in burnout rates of over ten points, according to *Mayo Clinic Proceedings*. It is too soon to know if this trend is simply a blip or a true improvement.[5] It is difficult to know if physicians are really adapting to all of these changes or, alternatively, institutions are acknowledging burnout and implementing solutions that are starting to have an impact. One other option is that burned out physicians are leaving healthcare or retiring early so that the numbers are skewed to show an improvement. It is hopeful that some of the initiatives and a new acknowledgment of the syndrome may drive change. Time will tell. Most studies still show an increasing or consistent rate of burnout throughout the healthcare system.

The trends of physician employment, electronic health record (EHR) adoption, enhanced documentation, increased regulations, and increasing time pressures have all been noted to be significant contributing factors to physician burnout. Physicians' training focuses on taking care of patients, with little emphasis on the administrative challenges in today's healthcare environment. Physicians are trained as individuals and are just learning the need for a team approach and leadership skills, which are now necessary. Team-based care has the potential to have a positive impact on both managing patient care and dealing with some of the challenging nonpatient activities. This will require a significant cultural shift both at the training level and practice level for physicians.

The challenge of today's healthcare environment is not only about additional work, and it is probably not really about work/life balance (although both are strong contributors). It is really about the administrative burdens that do not contribute to patient care and the frustration of false expectations on what delivering medical care should be. This juxtaposition of expectations in the practice of medicine versus the reality is part of this physician disillusionment or moral injury (as defined in Chapter 1). It is the new stresses and pressures that are not about patient care that fall out of line with the values of the practitioner. In today's practice of medicine, there are more and more administrative duties that do not add either directly or indirectly to the care of the patient. These include things such as typing into an EMR, getting approval for certain tests, and documenting items that could easily be done by clerical staff. Many of these factors are barriers to efficient and effective practice of good care (Figure 2.1).

Changes to Healthcare Last 10 Years

Hours worked	Same or increased
Work/Life balance	Still an issue (esp. millennials)
Autonomy	Decreasing
Paperwork	Increasing (EMR)
EMR challenges	New and increasing
Employment status	Now employed
Income	Decreased
Overhead	Increasing
Professional Respect	Decreased
Patient engagement with physician	Losing personal connections
Transparency	Increasing
Accountability	Increasing

Figure 2.1 Changes in healthcare in the last 10 years

Burnout at the Organizational Level

Burnout may not be obvious in an organization. If the organization is not looking for it or measuring it directly, the symptomatology may be indirect and perhaps even subtle. Things such as absenteeism, healthcare errors, staff turnover, the inability to fill new roles, physicians' bad behaviors, and many others may be core indicators. These indirect signs of physician burnout can be a result of the stresses, cynicism, and frustration that go with burnout. In this day and age, it is critical that each organization measure burnout on a regular basis using one of the recognized tools. It should be part of the CEO- and board-level dashboards. More on that later. From an organizational level, mitigating physician burnout can be a huge differentiator in an organization's ultimate success or failure. A more engaged physician and medical staff have positive financial implications as well as safety indications to the organization (see Figure 2.2).

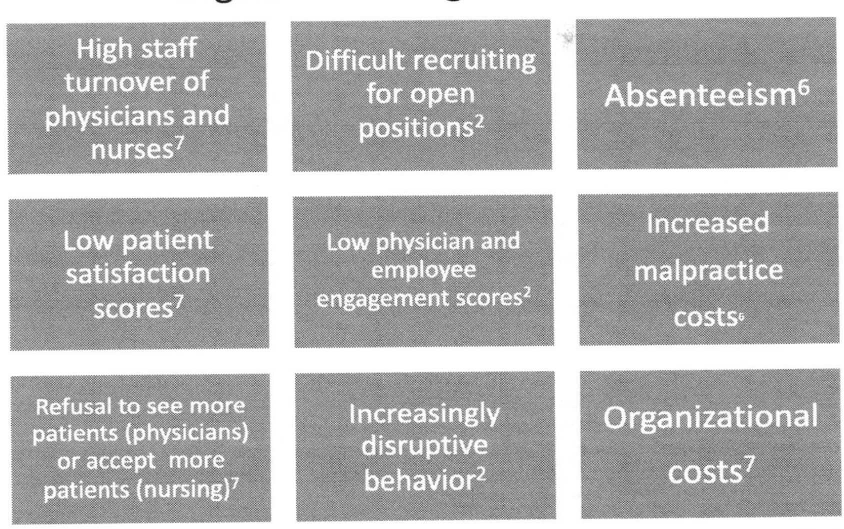

Organizational Signs of Burnout
High staff turnover of physicians and nurses7
Difficult recruiting for open positions2
Absenteeism6
Low patient satisfaction scores7
Low physician and employee engagement scores2
Increased malpractice costs6
Refusal to see more patients (physicians) or accept more patients (nursing)7
Increasingly disruptive behavior2
Organizational costs7

Figure 2.2 Subtle organizational signs of burnout

Burnout at the Individual Level

The same potential subtleties can also be true on a personal level. Often, burnout symptoms will present indirectly instead of as the key symptomatology of exhaustion, cynicism, and ineffectiveness. It will often be the spouse, family, or friends who see the symptoms first and may or may not understand the significance or the etiology. Physicians and healthcare workers are very good at hiding the symptoms at work. They are also very reticent to seek out help. Compounding this problem is the lack of easy access to resources that understand physicians and healthcare. The stigmata of a healthcare worker seeking mental health resources also has far-reaching consequences from the patient perspective, practice perspective, and licensing/credentialing perspective. These cannot be overstated.

Often the consequences of burnout are more obvious than the actual symptoms. Things such as substance abuse, broken relationships, lack of attention to detail, and depression

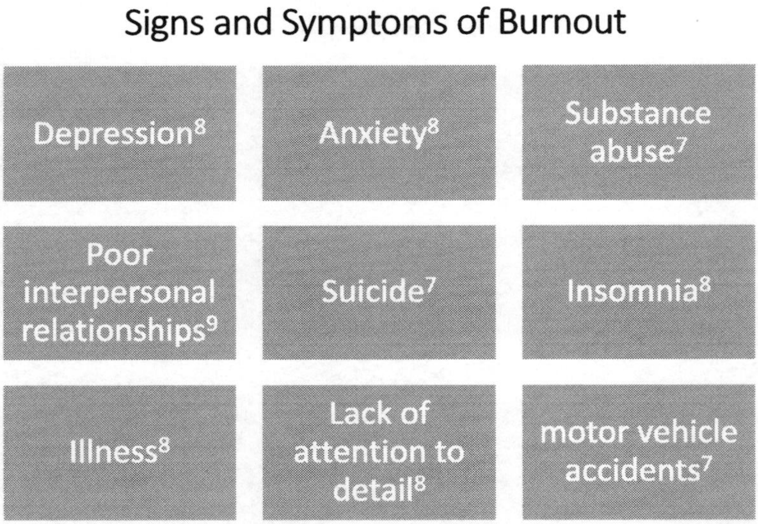

Signs and Symptoms of Burnout

Depression[8]	Anxiety[8]	Substance abuse[7]
Poor interpersonal relationships[9]	Suicide[7]	Insomnia[8]
Illness[8]	Lack of attention to detail[8]	motor vehicle accidents[7]

Figure 2.3 Personal signs and symptoms of professional burnout

can be more obvious on a personal level around family and friends, with burnout not always being the obvious etiology.[7] It is important for the family and friends to have some basic knowledge of the symptoms of burnout and to have a high-level suspicion since this can have significant personal consequences. If one looks at Figure 2.3, one sees some impactful symptoms including depression and suicide.

Moving toward Engagement

One solution to help mitigate the symptoms of burnout is to encourage your organizational staff to become more engaged. We will talk more about this in Chapter 12. With engagement you have physicians, nursing staff, and others actively engaged in patient-centric care and in making sure the organization is successful. An organization that has fostered engagement dramatically lowers the risk of their healthcare workers becoming burned out. The word "resiliency" also comes into play here. It has also been called "organization grit."[10] This resiliency, or

The Burnout / Engagement Spectrum
Burnout
Engagement
Exhaustion
High energy
Cynicism
Committed
Inefficient
Efficient
Adapted from Taris, W. Toon (2017) Burnout and Engagement: Identical Twins or Just Close Relatives, Sciencedirect 5 3-11

Figure 2.4 Burnout versus engagement

grit, helps an organization deal with some of the changes in healthcare. There is, of course, personal resiliency which protects each person at the individual level and when these are added up collectively help contribute to organizational culture and resiliency. It is a built-in reserve factor that helps resist the stresses and pressures leading to burnout. The interplay of the factors of burnout, resiliency, and engagement are all critical pieces in making sure an organization is healthy and thrives in the changing healthcare delivery models (Figure 2.4). Organizations must learn to adapt and quickly modify their strategies in this rapidly changing healthcare environment. This adaptability contributes to the resiliency and ultimately the long-term success of any organization.

Burnout Can Affect Everyone in Healthcare

Burnout affects everyone in healthcare, including medical students, interns, nurses, and any caregiver. Everyone throughout the healthcare continuum is subject to the same stresses to different degrees. It is very concerning that burnout can affect physicians and other healthcare workers so early in their career. This can lead to shortened careers and contribute to challenging organizational cultures. In this regard, if you have attendings and teaching staff that are burned out themselves, they can easily create a culture of burnout with their students

Burnout: High risk and low risk by specialty

High risk	Low risk
• Urology	• Nephrology
• Neurology	• Pathology
• Physical medicine and rehab	• Ophthalmology
• Internal medicine	• ENT
• Emergency medicine	• Plastic surgery
• Family medicine	• Dermatology

National Physician Burnout, Depression and Suicide Report 2019; *Medscape*
https://www.medscape.com/slideshow/2019-lifestyle-burnout-depression-6011056

Figure 2.5 Different specialties with different rates of burnout

and residents. This can create a vicious circle of burned out individuals creating more burned out students.

The people on the front lines are at the highest risk, and primary care physicians such as those in internal medicine and family practice are most at risk for the signs and symptoms of burnout. Please see Figure 2.5 to evaluate the different specialties and the risk of burnout.

Summary

Burnout is ubiquitous and impacts all healthcare workers including physicians, nurses, and residents. It has a very direct impact on physicians, healthcare workers, and their families as well as the organizations they support. Even though the symptoms may or may not be obvious, some of the signs at both the organizational and personal level are quite profound and impactful. It is critical that physicians, organizations, families, and others quickly recognize the signs and symptoms of burnout and move quickly to address the situation both on a personal level and longer term at the organization and societal level. The long-term effects of burnout to the delivery of healthcare cannot be overstated and it is important that the medical community, politicians and society recognize the dramatic impact and potential of this crisis. This must be addressed in an aggressive and proactive fashion.

Bibliography

1. Maslach, C., Schaufeli, W., & Leiter, M. (2001). Job burnout. *Annual Review of Psychology, 52*, 397–422.
2. DeChant, P., & Shannon, D.W. (2016). *Preventing Physician Burnout: Curing the Chaos and Returning Joy to the Practice of Medicine*. North Charleston, SC: CreateSpace Independent Publishing Platform.
3. Drummond, D. (2014). *Stop Physician Burnout: What to Do When Working Harder Isn't Working*. Charleston, SC: Heritage Press Publications.
4. Gooch, K. (2018). Why physician burnout jumped to 54% over 3 years. Retrieved from https://www.beckershospitalreview.com/workforce/why-physician-burnout-jumped-to-54-over-3-years.html.
5. Cheney, C. (2019). Physician burnout rate drops 10.5 points after spike. Retrieved from https://www.healthleadersmedia.com/clinical-care/physician-burnout-rate-drops-105-points-after-spike.
6. Cheney, C. (2018, June 21). Two kinds of interactions reduce physician burnout. *HealthLeaders Analysis*. Retrieved from https://www.healthleadersmedia.com/clinical-care/two-kinds-interventions-reduce-physician-burnout.
7. West, C.P., Dyrbye, L.N., & Shanafelt, T.D. (2018). Physician burnout: Contributors, consequences, and solutions. *The Association for the Publication of the Journal of Internal Medicine, 283*(6), 516–529.
8. Bourg, S. (2013, November 26). The tell tale signs of burnout . . . do you have them? Retrieved from https://www.psychologytoday.com/us/blog/high-octane-women/201311/the-tell-tale-signs-burnout-do-you-have-them.
9. Mindgarden physician burnout solutions. Retrieved from https://www.mindgarden.com/content/34-physician-burnout-solutions.
10. Lee, T.H., & Duckworth, A.L. (2018, September–October). Organizational grit – Turning passion and perseverance into performance: The view from the health care industry. *Harvard Business Review*, Sept-Oct issue, 98–105.

11. Taris, W.T., Ybema, J.F., & Beek, Iv (2017). Burnout and engagement: Identical twins or just close relatives? *ScienceDirect, 5*, 3–11.
12. Kane, L. (2019, January 16). Medscape national physician burnout, depression & suicide report 2019. Retrieved from https://www.medscape.com/slideshow/2019-lifestyle-burnout-depression-6011056.
13. Berg, S. (2019, March 19). How burnout in physicians compares to other professional degrees. Retrieved from https://www.ama-assn.org/practice-management/physician-health/how-burnout-physicians-compares-other-professional-degrees.
14. Cheney, C. (2019, March 25). Are your physicians suffering from burnout – Or Moral Injury? Retrieved from https://www.healthleadersmedia.com/clinical-care/are-your-physicians-suffering-burnout-or-moral-injury.
15. El-Aswad, N., Ghossoub, Z., & Nadler, R. (2017). *Physician Burnout: An Emotionally Malignant Disease*. North Charleston, SC: CreateSpace Independent Publishing Platform.
16. Khatri, B.O. (2018). *Healthcare 911: How America's Broken Healthcare System Is Driving Doctors to Despair, Depriving Patients of Care, and Destroying Our Reputation in the World*. Milwaukee, WI: Hansa House (in collaboration with Henschel HAUS).
17. Koeck, P. Difference between stress and burnout? Retrieved from https://www.15minutes4me.com/difference-stress/.
18. Kimmell, J. (2018, October 30). The 5 biggest risk factors for physician burnout, according to our, 13,371-physician survey. Retrieved from https://www.advisory.com/_apps/dailybriefing print?i={5A855D10-3247-42CF-B138-FAD00EF506B4}.
19. Larson, J. (2018, September 11). The leading cause of physician burnout. Retrieved from https://www.staffcare.com/the-leading-cause-of-physician-burnout/?utm_source=pardot&utm_medium=email&utm_campaign=sc-newsletter-9.20.18_st.
20. Surbhi, S. (2016, August 10). Difference between stress and burnout. Retrieved from https://keydifferences.com/difference-between-stress-and-burnout.html.
21. Wolf, M., & Gillis, S. (2017). *The Other Side of Burnout: Solutions for Healthcare Professionals*. Indianapolis, IN: Dog Ear.
22. Wong, A.V., & Olusanya, O. (2017). Burnout and resilience in anesthesia and intensive care medicine. *Oxford Academic, 17*(10), 334–340.

Chapter 3

Looking at Causality

George Mayzell

Contents

We will look at burnout through multiple lenses, focusing on three different areas. The first is the personal/professional physician viewpoint. The second is the institutional viewpoint, which is usually a hospital or health system. Last, we look at the societal and environmental etiologies of burnout.

Professional and Personal

It is naïve and unreasonable to blame the individual physician or healthcare provider for burnout. While it is true that there can be personal stressors and issues that contribute or make somebody susceptible to burnout, it is still fundamentally a systems issue for the most part. There are challenging causes and effects at play here. These personal issues can make an individual more susceptible to burnout, however challenges and stresses at work which contribute to burnout, can also exacerbate these personal issues. It is also true that some individuals are more resilient to the stresses of both work and home life than others. These are personality traits built into one's character through genetics and environment and it is not totally clear what makes a person more or less resilient to stressors.

For the most part burnout is a system- and societal-level problem that must be dealt with from that perspective. It was found that only 20% of burnout is from individual make-up and behaviors; the majority is system driven according to Dr. Sinsky.[1] The stressors involved in practicing medicine and all of the misalignment of administrative burdens are clearly the most impactful in creating burnout. it is important that we address these issues directly and not just focus on individual physician resiliency and/or stressors.

The personal side seems to get the most attention. There are a number of personal Yin and Yang pushes and pulls against a person's innate resiliency. The path to becoming a healthcare provider requires resiliency. It is impossible to go through a healthcare training system without some basic "grit."[2] This resiliency is counterbalanced by all the other stressors that come with a medical career. If one thinks about the challenges, effort, and energy that it takes to embark on a medical career there is obviously a self-selection process that identifies individuals that are resilient, dedicated and committed. It is a reasonable assumption that individuals that go through the tedious and challenging process of becoming a physician are more resilient. The first and most obvious are the innate challenges in work–life balance and the aggressive work schedule that is necessary in the health professions.

It is hard to believe that the work commitment in healthcare has changed that much over the last 20 years. It is more likely, at least in my opinion, that all the other things that we will discuss shortly pushed against this work-life balance and work schedule to create a mismatch of expectations versus reality, creating what we have termed "physician disillusionment" or "healthcare worker disillusionment."

I believe one of the most important influencers of this increasing mismatch is the loss of autonomy that has come with the new world of physician's practice. Physicians are now, more often than not, employees of large systems with non-physician managers.

One of the more appealing aspects of being a practicing physician is independence, with the autonomy and free rein of decision-making that it brings. With the advent of employees and "managed" care, many of these decision-making autonomous choices have gone away. Better patient communication has been shown to have a positive impact on physician burnout.[3, 4] One of the least appealing aspects of medicine, and a large contributor to burnout is all the administrative burdens that often act as barriers to patient care. This will be discussed in more detail in later chapters.

The risk of malpractice suits has ebbed and flowed but seems to be ever present. As anybody in the healthcare professions knows, this is a very personal issue. In most cases, it is not simply suing a hospital or institution; the suits are all personal and so are the emotions that go with it. The financial and legal ramifications of being sued personally can affect personal finances. The future is often in the crosshairs, as a pending lawsuit may influence medical staff reappointment or employment. This is certainly another stressor, particularly for physicians.

The next item is the erosion of the physician-patient relationship. The reason most physicians and other healthcare providers got into medicine is the physician-patient or healthcare worker-patient relationship. This has dramatically changed over the last several years. Currently, there are intensivists, hospitalists, SNFists, and others. Communication is poor, the handoffs are incomplete, and the physician-patient relationship is more episodic than it is longitudinal. If you think about it, it is almost like an assembly line more than any kind of relationship. The patient may see the primary care physician in the office and go to a specialist's office (often without communication) and then go into the hospital, where they are seen by a hospitalist and then on discharge seen by rehab physicians or other different specialties. The whole dictum of captain of the ship and care coordination is, unfortunately, more fiction than reality. New programs like patient-centered medical home and other team-based care initiatives are starting to mitigate lack or care coordination.

Another mitigating factor is the increasing use of advanced practice providers such as PAs and NPs. The issue is not whether we should be using these advance practice providers (APPs), but how we use them. Often APP's, rather than being part of a team-based care approach, are shuffled off to see either overflow or acute care patients. If they are in the hospital, they may not have any relationship with the primary care physician and only have relationships with hospitalists. Thus, there is no relationship formed with these physicians and the APPs. The relationship with the primary care or specialist provider may not be preserved in these clinic models (Figure 3.1).

Personal risk factors for burnout

- Have work life conflicts[5]
- Being younger than 55 years old[6]
- Females[6]
- Having children[7]
- Married to a physician[7]
- Being midcareer[5]
- Involved in malpractice case[8]

Figure 3.1 Personal risk factors contributing to burnout

Hospital/Delivery System

As physicians and other healthcare workers move from mom-and-pop shops of old into new employment models, this new paradigm is increasing the loss of autonomy to an already challenging situation. Many physicians become employed to get out from under some of the administrative headaches, as well as to finance their electronic medical records (EMRs). With well over 50% of primary care physicians now being employed by hospitals,[9] the paradigm is shifting, adding to the loss of autonomy and more burnout symptoms.

The administrative and clerical burden is becoming increasingly time consuming. There is no end in sight to the increasing administrative burdens. This can include everything from prior authorization and precertification for getting testing and drugs approved and even getting certain drugs approved inside the hospital by requiring specialty consults. All this can be very overwhelming and more important, takes time away from clinical care.

The hospital used to be a central meeting point for physicians. The camaraderie and sharing that were part of the physician lounge experience is evaporating. More primary care physicians and even many specialists are choosing to not go to the hospital and use hospitalists in their place. This is common in the area of primary care, but "specialty hospitalists" are becoming more prevalent. This decreases the opportunity for physician-to-physician interaction, which can be beneficial for physician camaraderie, but also important for patient care communication. In the past, many conversations about patient care were done in this informal fashion leading to better coordination of care. While there certainly may be benefits to these new models of care delivery, there are many communication challenges that need to be overcome. All of these can contribute to more fragmentation.

Medical societies and other formal and informal physician organizations were a large part of a physician's professional and personal social environment. The societies were an important part of the camaraderie and communication among various peer groups. In recent years, these societies have become less of a nidus for these important interactions.

Another challenge for physicians is the perception of a loss of fairness in these new healthcare delivery models. Often, non-physician executives and leaders are making important decisions about patient care and healthcare strategies. While they may not be affecting clinical care in a direct way, the decisions to open or close certain times for an MRI, to buy another's CAT scan machine, make available other high-end medical procedures, or even weekend staffing at the hospital have direct patient care applications. This also includes managed care organizations where getting approval for certain procedures and/or denial of payment can impact the care process. This inherent unfairness of non-physician executives making these kinds of decisions is very frustrating to physicians.

Another challenge is the overwhelming amount of information on the Internet. While there is much good information, there's also a lot of inaccurate information that must be dealt with. This misinformation and the plethora of information on the Internet can dramatically increase the communication time with patients and families. The competing challenge of physician time management in the office or hospital visits, while ensuring patient satisfaction, contributes to increased opportunities for stress and burnout. Certainly, all of us would want patients to be better informed with more accurate information. The challenges is that there is as much bad information as there is good, and it can be extremely time consuming for healthcare providers to refute these false claims and miracle cures.

Finally, there is the electronic medical record, or EMR. This will be discussed more in future chapters; however, there is much controversy about the current EMR. Most people believe that the EMR is designed well for billing and coding but not very well designed for patient care. It is difficult to get information out of it for day-to-day care decision-making and very difficult to put information into it. While one can argue about the benefits of EMR in terms of tracking and trending, drug interactions, and other alerts, it is generally felt by physicians that this takes too much additional time away from patients. Physicians spend up to 50% of their time looking at a computer screen when in the room with a patient.[10] The system must evolve dramatically to meet its potential. New artificial intelligence (AI) and other voice-activated solutions are on the long-term drawing board. We must look forward to a time when the electronic medical record not only improves patient care, but also minimizes administrative time and distractions.

Societal and Environmental

The biggest societal and environmental issue that we see affecting physicians and healthcare workers is the change in the respect that is given to them as professionals. Over the years, physicians have now become "providers" or in some cases, simply "PCPs." They are now employees of health systems and they are now often interchanged with all other healthcare providers. This issue affects the physician's value expectations when compared to the value realities.

Society also has different expectations of physicians from what it had in the past. In general, people now have more immediate expectations and just-in-time needs for treatment. There is no informational downtime, and expectations are 24/7/365. In concert with these expectations are new communication strategies such as Electronic visits (E-visits) and mobile health. Smart phones make it impossible to get away from the constant communication that is part of a medical delivery system. It can also lead to alert fatigue, making it difficult to separate true emergencies from false alarms.

In the near future, expectations will be that all "health" information is brought into the healthcare delivery space. This includes telehealth and telemedicine, wearables, and perhaps even social media information. There are many challenges ahead.

Bibliography

1. Berg, Sara (2017, November 2). To address burnout underlying causes, to team base care. Retrieved from https://www.ama-assn.org/practice-management/physician-health/address-burnouts-underlying-causes-look-team-based-care.
2. Lee, T.H., & Duckworth, A.L. (2018, September–October). Organizational grit – turning passion and perseverance into performance: The view from the health care industry. *Harvard Business Review*. Retrieved from https://hbr.org/2018/09/organizational-grit.
3. Henry, T.A. (2019, February 28). The key to tackling physician burnout: Listening to each other. Retrieved from https://www.ama-assn.org/practice-management/physician-health/key-tackling-physician-burnout-listening-each-other.
4. Berg, S. (2017, July 7). Better communication with patients linked to less burnout. Retrieved from https://www.ama-assn.org/practice-management/physician-health/better-communication-patients-linked-less-burnout.
5. Henry, Tanya Albert (2019, February 11). Physician burnout: 10 working factors that hinder your well-being. Retrieved from https://www.ama-assn.org/practice-management/physician-health/physician-burnout-10-work-factors-hinder-your-well-being.
6. West, C.P., Dyrbye, L.N., & Shanafelt, T.D. (2018). Physician burnout: Contributors, consequences, and solutions. *The Association for the Publication of the Journal of Internal Medicine, 283*, 516–529.
7. Rees, Laren (2015, August 7). 8 things that can put you at risk for burnout. Retrieved from: https://www.ama-assn.org/practice-management/physician-health/8-things-can-put-you-risk-burnout.
8. Beckers (2011, November 15). Malpractice lawsuits link to physician burnout, dissatisfaction. Retrieved from https://www.beckershospitalreview.com/news-analysis/malpractice-lawsuits-linked-to-physician-burnout-dissatisfaction.html.

9. Medscape family medicine physician lifestyle, happiness and burnout report 2019. Retrieved from https://www.medscape.com/slideshow/2019-lifestyle-family-medicine-6011113.
10. Cohen, Jessica Kim (2017, April 4). Study: Physicians spend 50% of their day on "desktop medicine". Retrieved from https://www.beckershospitalreview.com/healthcare-information-technology/study-physicians-spend-50-of-their-day-on-desktop-medicine.html.
11. Fred, H.L., & Scheid, M.S. (2018). Physician burnout: Causes, consequences, and cures. *Texas Heart Institute Journal*, *45*(4), 198–202.
12. Caliri, A. (2018, November 5). The root causes of physician burnout and practical options for addressing them. Retrieved from https://www.beckershospitalreview.com/hospital-physician-relationships/the-root-causes-of-physician-burnout-and-practical-options-for-addressing-them.html.
13. Runge, M.S. (2018, January 5). Opinion: It's time to treat physician burnout's root causes. Retrieved from https://labblog.uofmhealth.org/industry-dx/opinion-its-time-to-treat-physician-burnouts-root-causes.
14. Grinspoon, P. (2018, June 22). Physician burnout can affect your health. Retrieved from https://www.health.harvard.edu/blog/physician-burnout-can-affect-your-health-2018062214093.
15. Aldinger, K. (2018, February 11). Addressing the main cause of physician burnout. Retrieved from https://www.medicaleconomics.com/article/addressing-main-cause-physician-burnout.
16. Berg, S. (2019, March 19). How burnout in physicians compares to other professional degrees. Retrieved from https://www.ama-assn.org/practice-management/physician-health/how-burnout-physicians-compares-other-professional-degrees.
17. De Keyrel, A. (2017, February 3). The top 8 factors that cause physician burnout. Retrieved from https://www.mededwebs.com/blog/well-being-index/the-top-8-factors-that-cause-physician-burnout.

Chapter 4

Consequences of Burnout

George Mayzell

Contents

Burnout is thought to have severe consequences to both healthcare providers at the personal level and our current healthcare delivery organizations at the system level. Burnout of physicians, nurses, and other medical staff affects the day-to-day care that patients receive, including having a major impact on patient safety.

It also affects the efficiency of our systems as the capacity to handle increasing patient care demands of an aging population with potential physician shortages looms. The decreased effectiveness of the delivery system also has impact. The consequences of burnout are, perhaps, best broken down into four different categories: personal consequences, patient safety and experience, organizational impacts, and societal impacts.

Personal Consequences

Burnout has personal consequences for both physician and staff. These consequences include impacts at home and at the office (physician's office or the hospital). These issues start during medical school with students having a high rate of burnout (52.8%) and a much higher likelihood of unprofessional behaviors.[1] As we develop treatments and solutions we must remember to focus earlier and earlier in the healthcare training process.

There is also a higher prevalence of alcoholism and alcohol abuse, specifically documented with surgeons, but clearly affecting all providers. There is also an association showing a much higher rate of motor vehicle accidents.[2] The suicide rate is much higher than the general population with a particular emphasis on female physicians.[3, 4]

This disruptive behavior, stemming from one aspect of burnout, depersonalization, can have a direct impact on everyone in the office or hospital setting since physicians often set the tone culturally. These toxic cultures can often feed on themselves and are difficult to reverse. This negative behavior can often feed on itself and cause a vicious cycle of a negative culture both at home and at work. It is difficult sometimes to separate the consequences of burnout from the healthcare provider's personal life and from their professional life. It seems that the symptoms of burnout cross over and affect work/life balance. Higher divorce rates, depression, and motor vehicle accidents clearly accrue to the personal health side; however, things such as absenteeism, turnover, and others are on the professional side (see Charts 2.2 and 4.2). There is obviously a direct interaction between all of these items Figure 4.1.

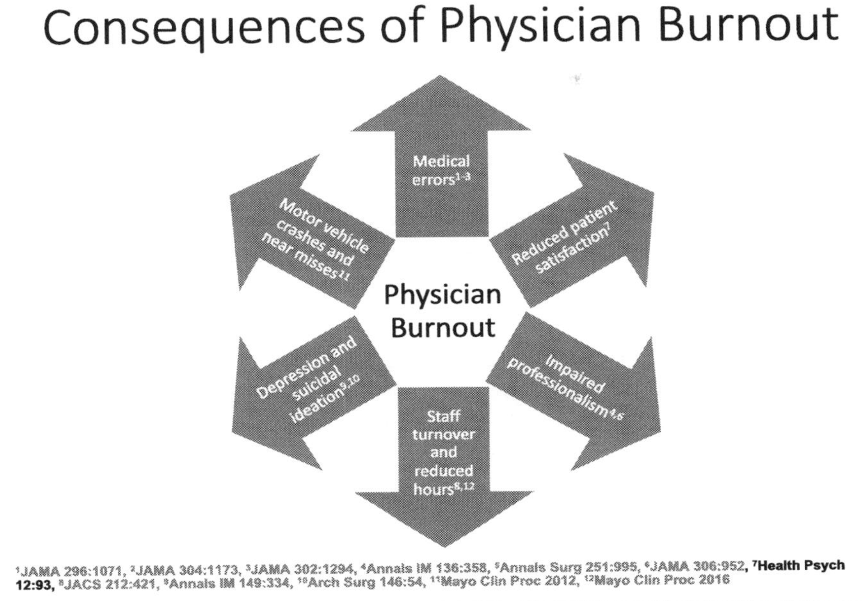

Consequences of Physician Burnout

Medical errors[1-3]

Reduced patient satisfaction[7]

Impaired professionalism[4,6]

Staff turnover and reduced hours[8,12]

Depression and suicidal ideation[9,10]

Motor vehicle crashes and near misses[11]

Physician Burnout

[1]JAMA 296:1071, [2]JAMA 304:1173, [3]JAMA 302:1294, [4]Annals IM 136:358, [5]Annals Surg 251:995, [6]JAMA 306:952, **[7]Health Psych 12:93,** [8]JACS 212:421, [9]Annals IM 149:334, [10]Arch Surg 146:54, [11]Mayo Clin Proc 2012, [12]Mayo Clin Proc 2016

Figure 4.1 Personal verbatims of burned out physicians

Patient Issues of Safety and Patient Experience

Burnout is a threat to patient safety because depersonalization results in poor interactions with patients. The rising need to complete tasks not directly focused on patient care, and often seen as bureaucratic by the caregivers, results in less time spent with patients and more time spent on "non-value-added" administrative burdens; this creates an ever-increasing sense of stress. In an article from the Mayo Clinic, 10.5% of physicians reported a major medical error in the prior three months, and, of these, the majority of physicians were more likely to have symptoms of burnout (77.6% versus 51.5%).[11]

There are clear links between physician and healthcare worker burnout and rates of errors.[12 13, 7, 8, 1]

There is also clear evidence of surgical errors related to stress and burnout.[5] With a clear association of stress, medical errors and behavioral issues related to burnout, and a burnout rate of over 50%, there is clearly a healthcare crisis.

The Cost of a Burned – Out Doc

- Physician burnout is costing the U.S. approximately 4.6 billion annually.[18]
- Cost of recruitment is $250,000 to a million.[19,21]
- Replacing a physician often cost 2 to 3 times their annual salary.[19]
- Burnout is costing organizations about $7,600 annually per employed physician.[18]
- Early retirement and reduction in clinical hours are also adding significant costs.[20]

Figure 4.2 Personal and patient consequences of burnout

We are only beginning to unpack the threat to quality and safety of our healthcare system that burnout causes. This may be one of the biggest threats to the quality and the integrity of our current medical delivery system[14] Figure 4.2.

Organizational

The organizational consequences of burnout are also significant. The first and most obvious one is the inherit conflict of burnout with workplace engagement and job satisfaction. Several studies link job satisfaction in the workplace directly to patient satisfaction results.[19]. Diminished job satisfaction contributes to a higher rate of physician and staff turnover, as well as difficulty filling positions. This can be incredibly costly.[20,21] The cost, in today's figures, has numbers as high as $1 million dollars for an organization to replace a primary care physician. This takes into account not only the time and cost of recruiting, but also the lost revenue while finding a new physician, getting him/her credentialed, and getting the practice ramped up to capacity.[16,18] These cost and time frames are only getting larger and longer. Clearly the system that figures out a way to manage this part of an institution's intrinsic culture can create wins by maintaining a consistent physician and nursing workforce. This may not only be a competitive advantage in the marketplace, but a necessary to survive.

Societal Impacts

At this point it seems obvious that there are societal impacts as well. We are already looking at facing a doctor shortage, especially in primary care. Physicians are retiring early, leaving the profession, cutting back on hours, and finding other ways of dealing with this mismatch in value/burnout.[1] This is not simply a local hospital or physician issue; it will have a stifling impact on everything from health and wellness of our society, access to healthcare, and workforce absenteeism/presenteeism. It is naïve to think that this can be solved at the individual physician or even individual institution level. There must be some major policy interventions and cultural shifts.

Bibliography

1. Dyrbye, L.N., Massie, S., Eaker, A. et al. (2010). Relationship between burnout and professional conduct and attitudes among US medical students. *JAMA*, *304*(11), 1173–1180.
2. West, C.P., Dyrbye, L.N., & Shanafelt, T.D. (2018). Physician burnout: Contributors, consequences, and solutions. *The Association for the Publication of the Journal of Internal Medicine*, *283*, 516–529.
3. Castellucci, M. Healthcare industry takes on high physician suicide rates, mental health stigma. Retrieved from http://www.modernhealthcare.com/article/20180929/NEWS/180929901.
4. Anderson, P. (2018, May 8). Doctors' suicide rate highest of any profession. Retrieved from https://www.webmd.com/mental-health/news/20180508/doctors-suicide-rate-highest-of-any-profession.
5. West, C.P., Huschka, Mashele, Novotny, P.J. et al. (2006). Association of perceived medical errors with resident distress and empathy: A prospective longitudinal study. *JAMA*, *296*(9), 1071–1078.

6. West, C.P., Tan, A.D., Habermann, T.M., Sloan, J.A., & Shanafelt, T.D. (2009). Association of resident fatigue and distress with mercy medical errors. *JAMA, 302*(12), 1294–1300.
7. Cheney, C. (2018, September 13). Physician burnout impacts safety, professionalism, patient satisfaction. *Health Leaders Analysis.* Retrieved from https://www.healthleadersmedia.com/clinical-care/physician-burnout-impacts-safety-professionalism-patient-satisfaction.
8. Shanafelt, T., Mongo, M., Schmitgen, J. et al. (2016). Longitudinal study evaluating the association between physician burnout and changes and professional work effort. *Mayo Clinic Proceedings, 91*(4), 422–431.
9. Cheney, C. (2018, June 21). Two kinds of interactions reduce physician burnout. *Health Leaders Analysis.* Retrieved from https://www.healthleadersmedia.com/clinical-care/two-kinds-interventions-reduce-physician-burnout.
10. Kopynec, S. (2018, May 1). Provider burnout and the risk about practice. *APA News.* Retrieved from https://www.aapa.org/news-central/2018/05/provider-burnout-and-the-risk-of-malpractice/.
11. Tawfik, D.S., Profit, J., Morgenthaler, T.I., et al. (2018). Physician burnout, well-being, and work unit safety grades in relationship to reported medical errors. *Mayo Clinic Proceedings, 93*(11), 1571–1580.
12. Shanafelt, T.D., Balch, C.M., Bechamps, G., et al. (2010). Burnout and medical errors among American surgeons. *Annals of Surgery, 251*(6), 995–1000.
13. Gooch, Tanya (2018, August 21). Why physician burnout jumped to 54% over 3 years, Beckers Hospital. Retrieved from https://www.beckershospitalreview.com/workforce/why-physician-burnout-jumped-to-54-over-3-years.html.
14. Henry, T.A. (2019, July 5). Burnout's mounting price tag: What it's costing your organization. Retrieved from https://www.ama-assn.org/practice-management/physician-health/burnout-s-mounting-price-tag-what-it-s-costing-your.
15. Berg, S. (2018, October 11). How much physicians burnout is costing your organization. Retrieved from https://www.ama-assn.org/practice-management/economics/how-much-physician-burnout-costing-your-organization.
16. Dewa, C.S., Jacobs, P., Thanh, N.X., & Loong, D. (2014). An estimate of the cost of burnout on early retirement and

reduction in clinical hours of practicing physicians in Canada. *BMC Health Services Research, 14*, 254.

17. Haas, J.S., Cook, E.F., Puopolo, A.L., Burstin, H.R., Cleary, P.D., & Brennan, T.A. (2000).Is the professional satisfaction of general internists associated with patient satisfaction? *Journal of General Internal Medicine, 15*(2), 122–128.
18. Misra-Hebert, A., Kay, D.R., & Stoller, J.K. (2004). A review of physician turnover: Rates, *Causes, and Consequences. American Journal of Medical Quality, 19*(2), 56–66.
19. Berg, S. (2017, November 17). At Stanford, physician burnout costs at least $7.75 million a year. Retrieved from https://www.ama-assn.org/practice-management/physician-health/stanford-physician-burnout-costs-least-775-million-year.
20. Buchbinder, S.B., Wilson, M., Melick, C.F., & Powe, N.R. (1999). Estimates of costs of primary care physician turnover. *The American Journal of Managed Care, 5*(11), 1431–1438.
21. Fahrenkopf, A.M., Sectish, T.C., Barger, L.K., et al. (2008). Rates of medication errors among depressed and burnt out residents: Prospective cohort study. *The BMJ, 336*(7642), 488–491.
22. Firth-Cozens, J., & Greenhalgh, J. Doctors' perceptions of the links between stress and lowered clinical care. *Social Science & Medicine, 44*(7), 1017–1022.
23. Lombardozzi, K. (2013, April 2). Physician burnout – A threat to quality and integrity. Retrieved from http://www.sccm.org/Communications/Critical-Connections/Archives/Pages/Physician-Burnout--A-Threat-to-Quality-and-Integrity.aspx.
24. Oreskovich, M.R., Kaups, K.L., Balch, C.M., et al. (2012). Prevalence of alcohol use disorders among American surgeons. *The Archives of Surgery, 147*(2), 168–174.
25. Shanafelt, T.D., Bradley, K.A., Wipf, J.E., & Back, A.L. (2002). Burnout and self-reported patient care in an internal medicine residency program. *Annals of Internal Medicine, 136*(5), 358–367.
26. West, C.P., Tan, A.D., & Shanafelt, T.D. (2012). Association of resident fatigue and distress with occupational blood and body fluid exposures and motor vehicle incidents. *Mayo Clinic Proceedings, 87*(12), 1138–1144.
27. Williams, E.S., Manwell, L.B., Konrad, T.R., & Linzer, M. (2007). The relationship of organizational culture, stress, satisfaction, and burnout with physician-reported error and suboptimal patient care: Results from the MEMO Study. *Health Care Management Review, 32*(3), 203–212.

Chapter 5

The Importance of Measuring Burnout

George Mayzell and Patricia S. Normand

Contents

Maslach Burnout Inventory (MBI)

Before we talk about how burnout is measured, we need to acknowledge the criticality of actually making this part of regular hospital metrics. This metric should be part of a balanced scorecard and measured on a regular basis, preferably yearly. It should be measured with a reliable tool, using the same tool each year, and the results should be shared with the medical staff, the hospital leadership, the board of directors, and other stakeholders.

We have shared with you the cost of burnout in presenteeism, absenteeism, and staff turnover as well as both the quality of care inside the hospital and personal issues in the home. Measuring burnout and acting on this measurement should be a corporate imperative and will be a competitive necessity to healthcare systems in the future.

The gold standard of measuring burnout is the Maslach burnout inventory (MBI). It has been over 25 years since its initial publication. There are 22 questions in this tool that use three general scales: emotional exhaustion (EE), depersonalization (DE), and personal accomplishment (PE).[1]

This MBI instrument focusing on burnout in healthcare is published by a company called Mind Garden, which is an independent psychological publishing company. There is a charge for the use of their services and scoring. If one uses the Maslach burnout toolkit, this is a combination of the MBI and a work–life survey (AWS) to create an assessment for burnout prevention and remediation for professionals. The work-life survey (AWS) measures aspects of the work environment that may contribute to burnout. These include:

- Workload
- Control
- Reward
- Community
- Fairness
- Values

The AWS is a companion piece to the MBI, and we will not discuss it further here.[2]

The MBI defines burnout as scoring in the high range (27 or more points) on EE, the high range (13 or more points) for depersonalization (DP), and in the low range (31 or fewer points) for personal accomplishment (PA) among professionals who serve people who are suffering.[3]

Maslach and colleagues' work supports the theory that burnout must include both EE and DP to be called burnout.[4]

While there is little question that the MBI is a very reliable tool, [3, 5, 6] it was really initially used as a research tool, and there are several issues that complicate the interpretation of the diagnoses for burnout. These issues center on appropriate cutoffs for burnout between the different categories and also the issue of whether burnout is an absolute diagnosis, that is, a dichotomy. Perhaps it is more a range of diagnoses with low burnout, medium burnout, and high burnout. This would make it a continuum, in which case, where would the cutoff points be?

This creates significant problems since often the various studies on burnout use different definitions and cutoffs and sometimes even different measurement surveys.

An example of using different definitions of burnout is that in one study, 46.9% scored high on EE, 34.6% high on DP, and 54.4% high on at least EE or DP. If the authors of this study had used a definition based on high EE *or* DP scores, they would have reported a burnout score of 54.4%. If the authors had used the recommended combination of high scores on both DP *and* EE, the burnout score would have been 34.6%. This assumes all who scored high on DP also scored high on EE. This is just one example of the complications of different cutoffs and different scoring systems.[4] It should be obvious how complicated the scoring system can be.

Some other investigators have actually combined the three scores in some form of mathematical equation to use as a diagnosis and/or cutoff for burnout. There is no consistent process for doing this; the original MBI manual shows a distribution of scores on a normative scale and divides them into thirds.[5]

There have been five prominent approaches to defining burnout for the MBI. These include:[6]

- The combination of high EE, high DP, and low PA
- High EE and/or high DP
- High levels of EE and/or DP combined with a low PA
- A high score on any of the three subscales
- High levels on the EE subscale only

Another issue that complicates this burnout discussion is that one of the requirements of the MBI is that be given to participants blinded, that is, they should not know that the instrument is meant to measure burnout. This will cause some bias and possibly skew the results. This is of course challenging in an era when physicians are acutely aware of burnout.

Single-Question Surveys

In many cases, the 22-question MBI is felt to be too long, and it was difficult to engage busy professionals in filling out the survey. In these cases, a single-item burnout measure (or sometimes a few questions) has been used. While they certainly provide meaningful information and some actionable items, there is much controversy on the accuracy of these shortened surveys relative to the full MBI. At this point, there is no high usage of these single-question surveys. [8–10].

Other Burnout Measurement Tools

AMA Mini Z

The AMA uses the Mini Z burnout assessment (by Mark Linzer, MD)[10] which is a ten-item, open-ended questionnaire assessing satisfaction, stress, burnout, work control, chaos, value alignment, teamwork, documentation, time pressure, electronic health record (EHR) use at home and EHR proficiency.

The Mini Z survey was derived from the Z clinical questionnaire (Z stands for zero-burnout program). This was adapted from the Physician Work Life Study (Linzer 2000, Williams 2001). There is a single-item burnout question adapted from Freeborn's tedium index[11] and has been validated externally against the MBI[12] with very good correlations (r equals 0.65). There is significant future work scheduled to continue validation of the Mini Z.

The Mini Z is part of the AMA program called "STEPS Forward." [TM,13] This program is a comprehensive program to help physicians avoid burnout and deal with burnout. Most of it is online and available to both AMA members and nonmembers.

Oldenburg Burnout Inventory[3, 14]

This is a 16-item survey that assesses physical, affective, and cognitive factors. It focuses on exhaustion and disengagement in both work and an academic context. Personal accomplishment is generally excluded. It has positive and negatively framed items and is in the form of a four-point Likert scale from strongly agree to strongly disagree.

The Oldenburg burnout inventory was developed in response to the MBI not having negatively worded items, and it is based on the job-demands resource model. So far, it has had limited use with limited validation studies and small sample sizes.

Bergen Burnout Inventory[3, 14]

This is a nine-item survey that measures burnout at work, assessing exhaustion and cynicism as well as a person's sense of inadequacy at work.

Copenhagen Burnout Inventory

The Copenhagen burnout inventory[3, 14–16] is a 19-item survey with both positive and negatively framed items. It covers three areas: the degree of physical and psychological fatigue and exhaustion, physical and psychological fatigue, and client-related burnout. There are multiple questions for each of these scales. Each dimension is evaluated as a continuous variable, and there are limited links to outcomes related to healthcare professionals.

Other Inventories That Are More Focused on Well-Being

Stanford Professional Fulfillment Index (PFI)[3]

This is a 16-item survey that covers burnout including work exhaustion and interpersonal disengagement as well as professional fulfillment. Responses are on a five-point Likert scale. Compared to the Maslach Burnout Inventory, the PFI burnout scale sensitivity was 72% and specificity was 84%.[3]

Well-Being Index[3]

This is a seven- or nine-item instrument with yes or no responses. The total score is calculated by adding the number of yes responses. In one sample of physicians and medical students, every one-point increase in score resulted in a stepwise increase in the probability of distress and the risk for adverse personal and professional consequences.

Physician Work/Life Study Single Item[3]

This is a single-item question that is embedded in the Mini Z. "Overall based on your definition burnout, how would you rate your level of burnout?" Responses include "I enjoy my work … I have no symptoms of burnout; occasionally I am under stress … but I don't feel burned out; I am definitely burning out and have one or more symptoms; the symptoms of burnout and experience will not go away." This measure was released in 2000 and correlates fairly well with the single item on the MBI on exhaustion (National County of medicine, action collaboration on clinical well-being).

Depression, Anxiety, and Sleep

There are also several measurement tools that do not measure burnout directly. These tools tend to focus on depression, anxiety, and sleep. With the clear linkages of these other factors to burnout, it is important to consider some of these tools as well. Measuring depression is critical, given that physician suicide rates are significantly higher than the general population. The Patient Health Questionnaire (PHQ– 9)[3] and Beck Scale[17] are used to measure depression, while the NIH PROMIS[18] measure depression, anxiety, and sleep.

The Patient Health Questionnaire – 9 (PHQ – 9)[3]

This is a self-reported component of the Prime MD Inventory. For each of the questions, participants answered whether during the last two weeks the symptoms have bothered them not at all, several days, for more than half the days, or nearly every day. This includes suicidal ideation screening as well. This study has a sensitivity and specificity of 88% for major depressive disorder, and the study results have been associated with medical errors, work hours, and productivity (National Academy of Medicine, Action Collaborative).

There are several other studies, particularly on the wellness side, with more being developed every day. The challenges, as noted previously, of creating a consistent model with consistent cutoffs that is usable across multiple systems is critical.

Ultimately, until we have a consistent model with comparative scoring, it will be difficult to agree not on whether burnout is a huge issue, but how big an issue it is and how well we are doing eliminating it.

Summary

It is critical to measure burnout in order to explore the components contributing to it on a local level. Interventions that are put in place without discerning what the particular institution needs are will probably fail. In addition, the goal should be not just alleviation of burnout, but a return to enjoying practicing medicine in a fulfilling way. Optimally, the focus would be on resilience, wellness, growth, and happiness rather than the absence of burnout. Interventions on an individual level, such as gratitude practices, cognitive behavioral approaches, relaxation techniques, communication skills, and mindfulness can be useful although some evidence would indicate that organizational approaches may be superior to individual interventions.[19,20] Even if we cannot totally eliminate burnout, we can focus on things that have a positive impact on promoting engagement, health, and wellness.

Bibliography

1. Maslach, Christina, Leiter, Michael P., & Schaufeli, Wilmer. (2008, May 24). Measuring burnout, cartright-c05, 85–108. Retrieved from https://www.wilmarschaufeli.nl/publications/Schaufeli/298.pdf.
2. Mindgarden. Retrieved from https://www.mindgarden.com/117-maslach-burnout-inventory.
3. Valid and reliable survey instrument to measure burnout, well-being, and other work-related dimensions. Retrieved from https://nam.edu/valid-reliable-survey-instruments-measure-burnout-well-work-related-dimensions/.

4. Eckleberry-Hunt, J., Kirkpatrick, H., & Barbera, T. (2018).The problems with burnout research. *Academic Medicine, 93*, 367–370.
5. Maslach, C., Jackson, S. E., & Leiter, M. P. (1996). *Maslach* (3rd 3d.). Palo Alto California: Consulting Psychologist Press.
6. Doulougeri, K., Georganta, K., & Montgomery, A. (2016). "Diagnosing" burnout among healthcare professionals: Can we find consensus? *Cogent Medicine, 3*, 1237605 1–10
7. West, C.P., Dyrbye, L.N., Sloan, J.A., & Shanafelt, T.D. (2009). Single item measures of emotional exhaustion and depersonalization are useful for assessing burnout in medical professionals. *Journal of General Internal Medicine, 24*, 1318–1321.
8. West, C.P., Dyrbye, L.N., Satele, D.V., Sloan, J.A., & Shanafelt, T.D. (2012). Concurrent validity of single-item measures of emotional exhaustion and depersonalization in burnout assessment. *Journal of General Internal Medicine, 27*, 1445–1452.
9. Knox, M., Willard-Grace, R., Huang, B., & Grumbach, K. (2018). Maslach Burnout Inventory and a self-defined, single-item burnout measure produce different clinician and staff burnout estimates. *Journal of General Internal Medicine, 33*(8), 1344–1351.
10. Mini, Z. Retrieved from http://www.eedsfiles.com/Activity_Files/033170194/4911.pdf.
11. Schmoldt, R.A., Freeborn, D.K., & Klevit, H.D. (1994). Physician burnout: Recommendations for HMO managers. *HMO Practice, 8*, 58–63.
12. Rohland, B.M., Kruse, G.R., & Rohrer, J.E. (2004). Validation of a single-item measure of burnout against the Maslach burnout inventory among physicians. *Stress and Health, 20*, 759.
13. STEPS ForwardTM. Retrieved from https://edhub.ama-assn.org/steps-forward/pages/about.
14. Stresscenter at UCSF, Burnout, stress measurement network. Retrieved from https://stresscenter.ucsf.edu/measures/burnout.
15. Vaerktoejer, Sporgerkema et al. Copenhagen burnout inventory–CBI. Retrieved from http://nfa.dk/da/Vaerktoejer/Sporgeskemaer/Sporgeskema-til-maaling-af-udbraendthed/Copenhagen-Burnout-Inventory-CBI.
16. Borritz, M., Kristensen, T.S. (2004, February). Copenhagen burnout inventory – CBI. Retrieved from http://nfa.dk/da/Vaerktoejer/Sporgeskemaer/Sporgeskema-til-maaling-af-udbraendthed/Copenhagen-Burnout-Inventory-CBI.

17. Beck depression inventory. Retrieved from http://www.minddisorders.com/A-Br/Beck-Depression-Inventory.html.
18. NIH Promis. Retrieved from http://www.healthmeasures.net/explore-measurement-systems/promis/intro-to-promis/list-of-adult-measures.
19. Wiederhold, Brenda, Pietro, Cipresso, Pizzioli, D. et al. (2018, July 4) Intervention for physician burnout: A systemic review. *Open Medicine (Wars)*, *13*, 253–263. Retrieved from https://www.ncbi.nlm.nih.gov/pmc/articles/PMC6034099/.
20. Panagioti, Maria, Panagopoulou, Efharis, & Bower, P. et al. (2017, February 1). Controlled interventions to reduce burnout in physicians: A systemic review and meta-analysis. JAMA Internal Medicine, *177*(2), 195–205. Retrieved from https://www.ncbi.nlm.nih.gov/pubmed/27918798.
21. Comas-Diaz, L., Luthar, S.S., & Maddi, S.R., et al. (2014). The Road to Resilience. American Psychological Association. Retrieved from https://www.apa.org/helpcenter/road-resilience.
22. Dyrbye, L.N., Trockel, M., Frank, E., et al. (2017). Development of a research agenda to identify evidence-based strategies to improve physician wellness and reduce burnout. *Annals of Internal Medicine*, *166*, 743–744.
23. Demerouti, E, Mostert, K, & Bakker, A. (2010). Burnout and work engagement: A thorough investigation of the independency of both constructs. *Journal of Occupational Health Psychology*, *15*(3), 209–222.
24. Demerouti, E., Bakker, A.B., Vardakou, I., & Kantas, A. (2003). The convergent validity of two burnout instruments: A multitrait-multimethod analysis. *European Journal of Psychological Assessment*, *19*(1), 12–23.
25. Dolan, E.D., Mohr, D., Lempa, M., et al. (2015). Using a single item to measure burnout in primary care staff: A psychometric Evaluation. *Journal of General Internal Medicine*, *30*, 582–587.
26. Freeborn, D.K. (2001). Satisfaction, commitment, and psychological well-being among HMO physicians. *Western Journal of Medicine 174*, 13–18.
27. Greene, A. (2012, October 22). Measuring physician burnout. Retrieved from https://www.advisory.com/solutions/survey-solutions/survey-says/2012/measuring-physician-burnout.
28. Heinemann, L.V., & Heinemann, T. (2017 March 6). Burnout research: Emergence and scientific investigation of a contested diagnosis. *SAGE Open* *7*(1), 1–12.

29. Halbesleben, J.R., & Demerouti, E. (2005). The construct validity of an alternative measure of burnout: Investigating the English translation of the Oldenburg burnout inventory. *Work Stress, 19*, 208–220.
30. Lall, M.D., Gaeta, T.J., Chung, A.S., et al. (2019). Assessment of physician well-being, part one: Burnout and other negative states. *Western Journal of Emergency Medicine, 20*(2), 278–290.
31. Maslach, C. and Jackson, S.E. (1981). The measurement of experienced burnout. *Journal of Occupational Behavior, 2*, 99–113.
32. McMurray, J.E., Linzer, M., Konrad, T.R., et al. (2000). The work lives of women physicians: Results from the physician work life study. *Journal of General Internal Medicine*, 15, 372–380.
33. Mayer, S. (2018, January). Burnout. Retrieved from https://stresscenter.ucsf.edu/measures/burnout.
34. Maslach, C., Jackson, S.E., Leiter, M.P., et al. Maslach Burnout Inventory (MBI). Retrieved from https://www.statisticssolutions.com/maslach-burnout-inventory-mbi/.
35. Miller, R.N. (2017, April 24). Measure, act on these 6 factors tied to physician burnout. Retrieved from https://www.ama-assn.org/practice-management/physician-health/measure-act-these-6-factors-tied-physician-burnout.
36. Moreno-Jimenez, B., Barbaranelli, C., Herrer, M.G., et al. (2012, December). The physician burnout questionnaire: A new definition and measure. Retrieved from https://www.researchgate.net/publication/287710966_The_physician_burnout_questionnaire_A_new:definition_and_measure.
37. McMurray, J.E., Linzer, M., Konrad, T.R., et al. (2000). The work lives of women physicians: Results from the physician work life study. *Journal of General Internal Medicine, 15*, 372–380.
38. Rotenstein, L.S., Torre, M., Ramos, M.A., et al. (2018). Prevalence of burnout among physicians: A systematic review. *JAMA, 320*(11), 1131–1150.
39. Schaufeli, W.B., Bakker, A.B., Hoogduin, K., et al. (2001). On the clinical validity of the Maslach Burnout Inventory and the burnout measure. *Psychology and Health, 16*, 565–582.
40. Shaikh, A. A, Shaikh, A., Rajesh, D., et al. (2019, February 19). Assessment of burnout and its factors among doctors using the abbreviated Maslach Burnout Inventory. *Cureus, 11*(2), e4101.
41. Surbhi, S. (2017, November 11). *Difference between stress and burnout*. Retrieved from https://keydifferences.com/difference-between-stress-and-burnout.html.

42. Schaufeli, W.B., Enzmann, D., Girault, N. (1993). Measurement of burnout: A review. In: Schaufeli, W.B., Maslach, C., Marek, T., eds. *Professional Burnout: Recent Developments in Theory and Research*. Philadelphia, PA: Taylor & Francis, 199–215.
43. Schaufeli, W.B., & Taris, T.W. (2005). The conceptualization and measurement of burnout: Common ground and worlds apart. *Work Stress,19*(3), 256–262.
44. Schaufeli, W.B., Leiter, M.P., & Maslach, C. (2009). Burnout: 35 years of research and practice. *Career Development International*, *14*(3), 204–220.
45. Schmoldt, R.A., Freeborn, D.K., & Klevit, H.D. (1994). Physician burnout: Recommendations for HMO managers. *HMO Practice*, *8*, 58–63.
46. Thomas, N.K. (2004). Resident burnout. *JAMA*, *292*(23), 2880–2889.
47. Trockel, M., Bohman, B., Lesure, E., et al. A brief instrument to assess both burnout and professional fulfillment in physicians: Reliability and validity, including correlation with self-reported medical errors, in a sample of resident and practicing physicians. *Academic Psychiatry*, *42*, 11–24.
48. Waddimba, A.C., Scribani, M., Nieves, M.A., et al. (2016). Validation of single-item screening measures for provider burnout in a rural health care network. *Evaluation & the Health Professions*, *39*, 215–225.
49. West, C.P., Dyrbye, L.N., Erwin, P.J., et al. (2016). Interventions to prevent and reduce physician burnout: A systematic review and meta-analysis. *The Lancet*, *388*, 2272–2281.
50. Williams, E.S., Manwell, L.B., Konrad, T.R., Linzer, M. (2007). The relationship of organizational culture, stress, satisfaction, and burnout with physician-reported error and suboptimal patient care: Results from the MEMO study. *Health Care Manage Review*, *32*(3), 203–212.
51. Waddimba, A.C., Scribani, M., Nieves, M.A., et al. (2016). Validation of single-item screening measures for provider burnout in a rural health care network. *Evaluation & the Health Professions*, *39*, 215–225.
52. West, C.P., Dyrbye, L.N., Sloan, J.A., & Shanafelt, T.D. (2009). Single item measures of emotional exhaustion and depersonalization are useful for assessing burnout in medical professionals. *Journal of General Internal Medicine*, *24*, 1318–1321.

53. West, C.P., Dyrbye, L.N., Satele, D.V., et al. (2012). Concurrent validity of single-item measures of emotional exhaustion and depersonalization in burnout assessment. *Journal of General Internal Medicine, 27*, 1445–1452.
54. Williams, E.S., Manwell, L.B., Konrad, T.R., & Linzer, M. (2007). The relationship of organizational culture, stress, satisfaction, and burnout with physician-reported error and suboptimal patient care: Results from the MEMO study. *Health Care Management Review, 32*(3), 203–212.
55. Waddimba, A.C., Scribani, M., Nieves, M.A., et al. (2016). Validation of single-item screening measures for provider burnout in a rural health care network. *Evaluation & the Health Professions, 39*, 215–225.
56. Williams, E.S., Manwell, L.B., Konrad, T.R., & Linzer, M. (2007). The relationship of organizational culture, stress, satisfaction, and burnout with physician-reported error and suboptimal patient care: Results from the MEMO study. *Health Care Management Review, 32*(3), 203–212.

Chapter 6

Individual Solutions

George Mayzell

Contents

It is estimated that 80% of burnout is driven by systems factors and only 20% is related to individual factors. This reinforces the fact that burnout cannot fully be resolved on an individual basis but, rather, must be attacked more systemically at both the institutional and societal levels.[1] Restated, burnout is not just happening because of how physicians take care of themselves, but it is happening because of all of the artificial impositions, such as the EMR, new employment models, and constant connectivity, being imposed on them by the care delivery model. That being said, let us take a deeper look at individual solutions and how they can be addressed.

Many would argue that physicians are some of the worst professionals for taking care of themselves. Working long hours while balancing family life and dealing in high-stress situations are not immediately conducive to good self-care. The contributing stressors were set up long before one begins to practice medicine. Instead, these stressors date back to the medical school application process and throughout the medical education system itself. Excessive school and later work demands adversely impact these self-care practices, which later erode one's personal resiliency and contribute to burnout.

Burnout Risk

- **Night or weekend call – 3 to 9% for each additional night/ weekend**
- **Work-related tasks at home – 2% increase for each additional hour worked**
- **Work/home conflict – 200%-250% increase in burnout**
- **ER medicine, internal medicine, neurology – 300% increase**
- **Private practice – 20% increase**
- **Incentive pay –130% increase in burnout compared to other salary models**
- **Midcareer physician – 25% increase**
- **Computer Physician Order Entry (CPOE)- 29% increase**
- **Career misfit with goals – 275% more likely**

https://www.ama-assn.org/practice-management/physician-health/physician-burnout-10-work-factors-hinder-your-well-being

According to Dike Drummond, MD, burnout includes a physical component, that is, exhaustion; emotional components, cynicism, and depersonalization; and a spiritual component, which is "I'm not really being effective."[3] It is important to address each of these components as we move forward to mitigating this pending crisis.

As we noted earlier, individual solutions are only partial solutions in fighting burnout. Certainly, individuals have different proclivities to burnout depending on their personality makeups as well as their environmental situations. Personal resiliency can go a long way toward combating the feelings of burnout. Individual initiatives are critical; however, one will quickly notice that many of these individual initiatives overlap directly with the institutional initiatives since often both the individual and the institution will have to be involved in solving the same problem.

Individual personality characteristics and character play a key role in burnout and personal resiliency. A high-risk profile is characterized by high neuroticism, low agreeableness, introversion, and negative affect. As with many things, burnout is a result of the conduct of a complex interaction between personal resiliency and personality traits and one's external environment.[4] Several studies have also related a negative effect on age to burnout. According to Spickard, burnout level is directly related to age, with younger physicians much more susceptible to burnout. Female physicians are also 1.6 times more susceptible to burnout than males.[5] Younger physicians have a higher probability of burnout, with physicians younger than 55 having double the risk.[6] Physicians who are married to non-physicians also have an increased burnout risk up to 23% higher.[6] (Author's note: This study is at odds with the study quoted in Figure 3.1 reminding us of this topic's challenges.)

There is some irony in the fact that the personality traits that tend to make one a good physician, such as empathy, interpersonal skills, and a strong desire to help others, are the same traits that may lead to burnout. Younger physicians, who may be more idealistic and have more compassion and empathy, are at higher risk for burnout.[7]

Let us turn our attention to some of the individual components that account for, and that can be managed as contributing elements of, burnout.

Self-Awareness

Perhaps at the top of the list of contributing factors is self-awareness, or self-insight. Having a good understanding of one's own feelings and environment and being able to objectively analyze go a long way to knowing when there is an issue and what the best solutions might be. Alternatively, one's family is often in an even better position to evaluate these situations. So, self-reflection, analysis, and awareness of burnout and its symptoms are critical to even starting the path to finding individual and systemic solutions.

Many physicians are functioning in either partial or complete burnout mode and a feeling of total isolation. As this condition of burnout increasingly comes to the forefront, ideally physicians will begin to realize that this is not an isolated issue but one that many, if not all, physicians are dealing with at one level or another at some time in their lives. This self-awareness and self-focus will go a long way toward looking at opportunities to potentially solve the problem and decrease some of the issues that are affecting healthcare today.

Along with the self-awareness is the importance of being aware of those around you. If you are only concerned with keeping yourself out of trouble, you will not be aware when a comrade or associate needs a lifeline. Physicians can play an important role in helping their colleagues solve this ubiquitous problem.[8]

Stress

Stress is a major contributor to physician burnout. When stress is reduced, physicians are happier, collaborate more with their peers, and communicate better with patients. All physicians experience some level of stress. Chronic, unrelieved stress is one of the key factors that lead to physician burnout.

Some of the obvious things that we should be doing every day (and things that we recommend to our patients), include:

- Sleeping better, eating better and more balanced meals

- Engaging in daily physical activity
- Socializing, taking vacations, and having dedicated downtimes. Having time for hobbies or spiritual activities is also important
- Having a best friend or a peer to talk with
- Having one's own primary care physician

Physician Workload

One of the critical contributors to burnout is workload. This includes excessive workloads such as long work hours, frequent overnight call duties, and high-work intensity. This also involves work/life balance and a contributing loss of support from colleagues and others.

There's an independent relationship between burnout and work hours, with 3% increased odds of burnout for each additional hour worked per week. Night or weekend call duties increase the odds (for each additional day) by 3 to 9%. Time spent at home for work-related tasks result in a 2% increase in odds for each additional hour per week (think about all that electronic medical record (EMR) "pajama time").[6]

Physician Engagement and Focus

This can decrease burnout by focusing the work time on things that physicians enjoy doing. This is less stress provoking and allows more autonomy, particularly as it relates to work/life balance. Time off can be an important piece of a solution; however, the time off must be a total removal from job stressors. Vacation time is a critical piece of preventing burnout; however, in and of itself it is not enough to solve burnout for most individuals. Often, the workload is very high on return from vacation. The same stressors are right there on return from vacation. In our opinion, that must change.

Another important contributor to workload is making sure the institution or office is adequately and fully staffed. Staff shortages, vacancies, and overlapping vacations can dramatically alter the workload. Institutions that are chronically understaffed increase workloads, which contributes to burnout.

Work Efficiency

A large category that has significant overlap with organizational etiologies of burnout is the idea of workplace inefficiencies. While most of these must be fixed at the organizational level, there are many that can be fixed at the individual level. These include things such as time management, setting up the appropriate workflows, and creating macros/templates within the EMR. Working with EMR support liaisons can contribute to becoming a work expert (superuser) on the EMR.

One important aspect of this efficiency is looking at a predominately team-based care model. By allowing staff to perform some of the EHR duties and having everybody working at the top of their licenses, the physician can do what he or she was originally trained to do: take care of patients. It is impossible for a single physician provider to do everything him- or herself, and, therefore, working in a team-based atmosphere can have a huge positive impact on creating efficiencies.[9] For many, this team-based approach is foreign to how they were selected and trained as physicians.

The opposite of work efficiency is a chaotic workplace. While there are certainly people who thrive in chaos, most people find it frustrating and it contributes to the potential for burnout.[10]

The Infamous EMR

There will be an entire chapter dedicated to the EMR since it is such a significant issue; however, since the EMR is not going away, the key is to make it as efficient as possible. Use of the computerized physician-order entry has been associated with 29% greater rates of burnout.[11] Much of the solution lies at the corporate or system level. However, one can become a master of one's own knowledge of the EMR and create efficiencies by becoming a true expert or superuser of your own EMR. This includes setting up the appropriate shortcuts, macros, and other tricks of the trade that can help make your personal journey working with EMRs and patient care tolerable.

Other work inefficiencies include how one manages one's schedule and the control taken to working at the top of your license and delegating and managing nonessential workflow processes. There will be more on this in the chapter on systemic and environmental opportunities.

Regaining Control

Another large area of opportunity is to try to reclaim some of the "loss of control" from physicians, healthcare workers, and the challenge of clinical leadership. This issue overflows into some of the practice management and hospital management programs; however, trying to gain back some control of one's own schedule and one's own time is a critical piece.

Having control leads to less stress, which is an important internal component in helping physicians manage potential burnout. This probably also bleeds into the area of respect and expectations as a professional.

There have also been some correlations with the leadership style of one's boss. This is not unexpected and probably goes toward the organizational culture.[12, 13]

Regaining the Meaning of Work

Another component of self-healing is trying to find better ways to deal with the stress of healthcare delivery and the "loss of meaning" in our delivery of healthcare. Stress is certainly a component of everyone's life, and in healthcare it is perhaps more dominant. The challenge with burnout is that there is virtually no time to recover since the stress is omnipresent.

The struggle to find meaning in work is illustrated by the findings that physicians who spent less than 20% of work effort on the activity that they found most personally satisfying were three times more likely to be burned out than those who did not.[14]

One other area of regaining control is focusing back on the patient. When you talk to physicians, it is not the patient interactions that frustrate them; it is all the stuff that interferes with patient care. One of the things that has been shown to help physicians alleviate burnout is better communication. This communication with patients is a patient-centered communication that can decrease medical errors and increase the physician's joy at work. The relation between the clinician's level of satisfaction and the ability to build good rapport with patients is critical to staving off burnout, according to Dr. Aronson. These skills can be acquired through education and training.[15]

While not the exact opposite, clearly physician engagement is an opposing element compared to burnout. One of the proxies for physician engagement is that of physician leadership. Allowing oneself time and inclination to become involved in change and help to lead either at the institution or practice level is beneficial. This leadership also gives a sense of regaining control for both the physician and their peers and can contribute to getting a better sense of why they went into healthcare. The challenge is that physicians are not trained in leadership and, during their training, leadership was usually top down. Again, in our opinion, leadership is a skill set that physicians must learn and embrace.

Small-group programs have proven to be highly successful. These can be carried out at restaurants, physicians' houses, and can be hospital supported or supported by the medical staff.[6]

Creating a New Culture

It is about creating a new culture that is physician and health-care worker supportive and inclusive in decision-making. This may include an aggressive onboarding process for new physicians, including a mentorship relationship. It is critical for them to identify their passions and that they be allowed to focus on that which gives them meaning.[16]

Things that can help build a culture:

- Engage physician and nonphysician leaders as a leadership group to help guide the culture and work experience
- Encourage sharing of positive stories and themes throughout the organization
- Incorporate "appreciative inquiry" in the daily work
- Measure culture and share results with entire staff
- Encourage transparency
- Encourage peer-to-peer assistance
- Encourage self-awareness and helping peers

Social Context and Peer Support

Many hospital systems, including Mayo Clinic, are encouraging physicians to meet in small groups. Some of these are in physicians' homes; some are in restaurants. These are important events. In past years, physicians would have a chance to meet, talk, and commiserate in the physicians' lounge, usually before hospital rounds. Now many physicians do not go to the hospital and the ones that do often do not have much time to spend in physician lounges. This time to commiserate has gone away.[17, 18]

At Stanford in California, physicians are allowed to bank hours that they can then trade with each other. This gives them additional flexibility.[17] Many hospitals are also hiring chief wellness officers, not only to emphasize the importance of health, but also to help lead some of this cultural change.

Another area of successful intervention is physician peer coaching. Cleveland Clinic has emphasized this. This can be done at onboarding, when an experienced peer coach is assigned to a new physician joining the program. It can also be used later in the course of a career when dyads of physician leaders and hospital administrative leadership can be paired up to help act as support and change agents.[19]

Summary

These are some of the individual interventions that are effective in combatting burnout:

- Measure burnout and share results on a regular basis
- Help medical students to make informed specialty choices
- Look at efficiency and skills training
- Consider stress management and resiliency training
- Engage in physician small-group activities
- Educate physicians about burnout
- Implement stress reduction and mindfulness programs
- Implement team-based care approaches
- Manage work: consider part-time status, mandatory vacations
- Ensure that workload is equitable
- Encourage individuality among faculty and leadership
- Manage excessive workload: consider duty hour limits, appropriate job role descriptions, and fair productivity goals
- Commit to faculty and staff wellness training
- Advocate for fairness and transparency to medical staff
- Work efficiently: think about team-based care processes, prioritize, and delegate
- Balance work and home life: evaluate priorities and plan accordingly

- Provide opportunities for professional and leadership development
- Allow opportunity for shared decision-making and involvement of physicians in all relevant matters
- Optimize EMRs: become an expert and utilize all tricks of the trade; consider scribes and other resources
- Regain control: consider stress-management training, embrace mindfulness and positive coping strategies
- Regain meaning from work: focus on the things that satisfy you at work, participate in small-group activities with other physicians to share experiences

There is certainly a long list of things that physicians and other healthcare personnel can do to mitigate burnout on a personal basis. It is important to remember that the most effective initiatives must be done from a broader perspective. Corporate and organizational initiatives can be highly effective and can set the stage for physician and healthcare worker engagement and limiting burnout. There are of course additional things that can be done from a more global view point such as policy and societal changes. We will address these in future chapters.

Bibliography

1. Berg, S. (2017, November 2). To address burnout's underlying causes, look to team-based care. Retrieved from https://www.ama-assn.org/practice-management/physician-health/address-burnouts-underlying-causes-look-team-based-care.
2. Henry, TA (2019, February 11). Physician burnout: 10 work factors that hinder your well-being. Retrieved from https://www.ama-assn.org/practice-management/physician-health/physician-burnout-10-work-factors-hinder-your-well-being.
3. Drummond, D. Physician burnout – pathophysiology and treatment of burnout. Retrieved from https://www.thehappymd.com/blog/bid/290248/physician-burnout-pathophysiology-and-treatment-of-burnout.

4. Wiederhold, B.K., Cipresso, P., Pizzioli, D., Wiederhold, M., & Riva, G. (2018, July). Intervention for physician burnout: A systematic review. *Open Medicine, 13*, 253–263.
5. McMurray, J.E., Linzer, M., & Konrad, T.R. (2000, June). The work lives of women physicians results from the physician work life study. The SGIM career satisfaction study group. *Journal of General Internal Medicine, 15*(6), 372–380.
6. West, C.P., Dyrbye, L.N., & Shanafelt, T.D. (2018). Physician burnout: Contributors, consequences and solutions. *Journal of Internal Medicine, 283*(6), 516–529.
7. Weiderhold, B. (2018). Intervention for physician burnout: A systemic review, 2018. *Open Medicine, 13*, 253–263. Retrieved from https://www.ncbi.nlm.nih.gov/pubmed/29992189.
8. Berg, S. (2018, August 30). How to recognize and respond to burnout in a fellow physician. Retrieved from https://www.ama-assn.org/practice-management/physician-health/how-recognize-and-respond-burnout-fellow-physician.
9. Berg, S. (2018, September 17). Burned out? You're not alone. Here's how 2 doctors overcame it. Retrieved from https://www.ama-assn.org/practice-management/physician-health/burned-out-you-re-not-alone-here-s-how-2-doctors-over came-it.
10. Linzer, M., & Guzman, L., & Poplau, S. Physician burnout, AMA steps forward. Retrieved from https://amaalliance.org/wp-content/uploads/2019/01/preventing_physician_burnout-steps forward-ama.pdf.
11. Shanafelt, T.D., Dyrbye, L.N., & Sinsky, C. et al. (2016). Relationship between clerical burden and characteristics of the electronic environment with physician burnout and professional satisfaction. *Mayo Clinic Proceedings*, *91*(7), 836–848.
12. Shanafield, T.D., Balch, C.M., & Bechamps, G.J. et al. (2009). Burnout and career satisfaction among American surgeons. *Annals of Surgery*, *250*(3), 463–471.
13. Siu, C., Yeun, S.K., & Cheung, A. (2012). Burnout among public doctors in Hong Kong: Cross-sectional survey. *Hong Kong Medical Journal = Xianggang Yi Xue za Zhi*, *18*(3), 186–192.
14. Dewa, C.S., Loong, D., Bonata, S., & Trojanowski, L. (2017). The relationship between physician burnout and quality healthcare in terms of safety and acceptability: A systemic review. *BMJ Open*, *7*, E015141.

15. Berg, S. (2017, July 7). Better communication with patients linked to less burnout. Retrieved from https://www.ama-assn.org/practice-management/physician-health/better-communication-patients-linked-less-burnout.
16. Berg, S. (2019, April 10). Leadership development may be linked to reduced burnout rates. Retrieved from https://www.ama-assn.org/practice-management/physician-health/leadership-development-may-be-linked-reduced-burnout-rates.
17. Berg, S. (2018, December 3). 9 major institutions create healthier environment for physicians. Retrieved from https://www.ama-assn.org/practice-management/physician-health/9-major-institutions-create-healthier-environment-physicians.
18. Berg, Sara. Four lessons mayo clinic learn from group meetings to cut burnout: American Medical Association. Retrieved from https://www.ama-assn.org/practice-management/physician-health/4-lessons-mayo-clinic-learned-group-meetings-cut-burnout.
19. Berg, S. (2019, January 28). Cleveland clinic's doctor peer coaches build physician resiliency. Retrieved from https://www.ama-assn.org/practice-management/physician-health/cleveland-clinic-s-doctor-peer-coaches-build-physician.
20. Berg Sara. (2017, October 11). Taming clinical chaos means fewer physicians eyeing exit: Study: American Medical Association. Retrieved from https://www.ama-assn.org/practice-management/sustainability/taming-clinical-chaos-means-fewer-physicians-eyeing-exit-study.
21. Berg, S. (2017, July 5). Burnout's causes, fixes need rigorous research, says expert panel. Retrieved from https://www.ama-assn.org/practice-management/physician-health/burnouts-causes-fixes-need-rigorous-research-says-expert-panel.
22. Berg, S. (2017, July 12). On the road to burnout? How to set a different course. Retrieved from https://www.ama-assn.org/practice-management/physician-health/road-burnout-how-set-different-course.
23. Butcher, L. (2017, September 20). Solving physician burnout: Physician burnout is a multifaceted problem requiring collaborative solutions. Retrieved from https://www.hhnmag.com/articles/8584-solving-physician-burnout.
24. Girgis, L. (2018, December 30). Solving physician burnout requires so much more than self-care. Retrieved from https://www.kevinmd.com/blog/2018/12/solving-physician-burnout-requires-so-much-more-than-self-care.html.

25. Henry, T.A. (2017, May 10). Burnout: 6 boosters for research to improve physician well-being. Retrieved from https://www.ama-assn.org/practice-management/physician-health/burnout-6-boosters-research-improve-physician-well-being.
26. Henry, Tanya Albert. (2019, February 11). Physician burnout: 10 working factors that hinder your well-being. Retrieved from https://www.ama-assn.org/practice-management/physician-health/physician-burnout-10-work-factors-hinder-your-well-being.
27. Henry, T.A. (2019, February 28). The key to tackling physician burnout: Listening to each other. Retrieved from https://www.ama-assn.org/practice-management/physician-health/key-tackling-physician-burnout-listening-each-other.
28. Linzer, M., Visser, M.R.M., Oort F.J., et al. (2001). Predicting and preventing physician burnout: Results from the United States and the Netherlands. *The American Journal of Medicine*, *111*(2), 170–175.
29. Samuels, M.A. (2016, March 20). The antidote to physician burnout: A nine step program. Retrieved from https://thehealthcareblog.com/blog/2016/03/20/the-antidote-to-physician-burnout-a-nine-step-program/.
30. Staff News Writer. (2018, November 27). How to beat burnout: 7 signs physicians should know. Retrieved from https://www.ama-assn.org/practice-management/physician-health/how-beat-burnout-7-signs-physicians-should-know.
31. Patel, Rikininkumar, Bachu, Ramya A., Adikey, A., et al. (2018, November). Factors related to position burnout and its consequences: A review. *Behavioral Sciences*, *8*(11), 98.

Chapter 7

Organizational Solutions to Burnout

George Mayzell

Contents

As stated before in Chapter 6, there is much overlap regarding the personal solutions to burnout and the systemic solutions to burnout. In an ideal world, personal solutions and corporate/organizational solutions would be combined for a synergistic effect. As noted before, 80% of the solutions must be driven by the organization and societal changes.[1]

The first and probably the most important part of burnout from an organizational point of view is to acknowledge that it is real, that it is impactful, and that overcoming it must be an organizational imperative. While the cost of burnout is still being fully evaluated, recent estimates say that the cost of burnout to the United States is approximately $4.6 billion annually.[2] It costs anywhere from $500,000 to $1 million to recruit a new physician.[3, 4] Burnout is costing organizations about $7,600 annually per employed physician.[2] Furthermore, the cost of burnout both internally and socially is just starting to be measured, not just in turnover but in terms of workforce effectiveness metrics such as absenteeism and presenteeism. Hence, from an organizational perspective avoiding burnout is far from an academic or altruistic consideration – it is instead an imperative.

To address the issue, it is best brought to the forefront of discussions in a transparent manner and resourced accordingly. The status of burnout within any organization should be measured to establish a baseline with a commitment to remeasure on a regular basis. This remeasurement also must be shared with all staff in an open and transparent way. Once measured, interventions need to be put in place and resourced appropriately. Initiatives such as a wellness committee, a physician leadership committee, and a chief wellness officer are some examples. It needs to be built into the organization's culture and, more specifically, into the quality improvement model with a regular metric presented at both the staff and board levels.

Recapping:

- Burnout should be measured and reported on a regular and consistent basis.
- There should be annual reviews of supervisors.
- There should be dedicated leadership and supporting resources to address burnout.
- There should be open dialogue with physicians and hospital leadership on a regular basis regarding physician well-being/burnout.[5]

As stated above, we believe this to be a huge corporate imperative that carries large corporate risk. Conversely, if a corporation can master or at least mitigate burnout, we believe it can become a competitive advantage by lowering costs, improving quality, and creating a productive culture.

Electronic Medical Record

One of the most critical pieces contributing to burnout at the organizational level and, therefore, a critical place in which to place resources is mitigating the time, energy, and complexity of managing the electronic medical record (EMR) system. It seems as if on a regular basis additional tasks are added into the EMR system, which burdens the provider, resulting in longer days and less fulfilling work. How many times have we heard, "It's only one more click"? Physicians are now doing increasing amounts of administrative work that prior to this was done by office and hospital personnel. It can take 32 clicks to order and record a flu shot, and some studies show that doctors spend about two hours of paperwork for every hour they devote to patient care.[6] Since we are dedicating Chapter 8 to the EMR, we will leave the details to that separate discussion. Suffice it to say that acknowledging the EMR as a huge source of inefficiency and that mitigation strategies for both the physician and the organization are paramount.

Work Hours and Time Off/Work/Life Balance

Physicians and healthcare workers have always worked long hours. So, while this is clearly an important predictor of burnout, we believe the new variable is not the intensity nor duration of the work day, but rather the type of work that is being done. Much of it is administrative and not necessarily "added value" to patient care from the physician's perspective.

Things are also faster paced with much more connectivity, more data, more research, and more communication capabilities than have ever existed in the history of the world. No one is really off work since our smart phones, laptops, and tablets are so available. Productivity has also become a focus, whether in the employment model or not. If unfair productivity metrics are assigned, this adds to increasing stress and burnout as an external factor beyond "just delivering good care one patient at a time."

It is also typical for physicians to bring work home. This is particularly true of finishing up charts in the EMR system. This is been coined "pajama time."[7] It has been suggested that two to three hours a day is typical for "pajama time." In our view, this is unacceptable and not sustainable.

Another aspect of work/life balance is the idea of schedule flexibility. Physicians used to have more control over their time and were able to take time off for family and personal events. This is harder in the employed model as expectations change in this new model.

The most critical factor leading to burnout is the incredible time pressure that physicians and healthcare workers feel. They remain committed to great patient care but feel the pressures of the additional administrative, economic, regulatory, and compliance-related tasks that they are expected to do. It has been shown that compensation models that are not productivity driven have a huge benefit in not promoting burnout.[8]

So, what can be done about work/life balance? First of all, we have to ensure that workload expectations are reasonable and that any metrics or incentives are also reasonable. We need to give physicians control over the work schedule with flexibility. Team-based care will also help with some of this balance.

Team-based care has been proven to be very effective. This includes allowing staff to perform much of the Electronic Health Record work and allowing physicians to focus more directly on patient care. Also, team-based care has been shown to be extremely helpful when an extended care team was created to focus on these complex patients who had high-service needs. This might include an extended care team such as case managers, clinical pharmacists, diabetes educators, and high-risk care coordinators.[9] This allowed everybody to work together and to become more efficient.

The other thing that has been proven very effective is a different type of team-based care that focuses on the physician and healthcare worker. This includes assisting in life challenges, such as helping out in the day-to-day chores like picking up laundry, food shopping, cleaning their homes, using home food delivery services, and other errands.

This can also take the shape of time banking, as used at Stanford Medicine. This allows physicians to bank the time they spend doing underappreciated work such as mentoring, serving on committees, covering colleagues shifts where they earn credits that can be used for home-related services, such as meal delivery and dry cleaning[10] (Figure 7.1).

Five organizational engagement factors with negative correlation to burnout

- supports work life balance correlation of (.56)
- Is open/responsive to my input correlation of (.42)
- I have the right amount of autonomy correlation of (.41)
- Exec team shares the goals of clinicians correlation of (.41)
- Recognizes clinicians for excellent work *correlation of (.40)*

Adapted from Kimmel, J, (October 2018) the five biggest risk factors for physician burnout, according to our 13,371 – physician survey, daily briefing print the advisory Board Company

Figure 7.1 Organizational engagement factors

Leadership and Inclusiveness

Physicians are not typically trained as leaders; it is not part of the medical school curriculum. Also, until recently, physicians were not trained in team-based care models either. All this is to say that the new reality of healthcare delivery requires new and different skill sets. We believe that a strong organizational lever that can be pulled to substantially affect burnout relates to physician engagement and, more specifically, inclusiveness. This can be as a physician contributor or as a leader. More physicians are stepping into leadership roles, and this is important in helping mitigate burnout, but it is also important in working within the professional industry to help their peers to improve the burnout culture. Leadership, as well as engagement from the rank-and-file physicians and healthcare workers, is critical to understand what needs to be changed, and also how it needs to change. In the future, it will be critical to balance cost, quality, outcomes, and patient experience and be able to make patient-centric decisions.

Physician Professionalism

Professionalism is a challenge. We are at an age in which independent physicians and practitioners are now becoming employed in large hospital systems, and the insurers are now calling physicians providers and lumping them into groups with physician assistants and nurse practitioners. In some ways, we could argue that it is physicians' fault that we have lost some of their own professionalism and become more disengaged.

Physicians have lost their edge regarding professionalism. Our medical societies have all but died out, and, just based on participation, the AMA is struggling to represent physicians. We have lost a common voice and specialty societies have become our voice. We have become more disengaged in the process and have allowed others to try to fix what is a broken system. In one study "an organization which recognized clinicians for excellent work" had a negative correlation of 0.4.[11]

Loss of professionalism is not an easy problem to solve at the organizational level. To some degree, physicians must solve this problem themselves by insisting on being treated as professionals. This is a challenge in a world of primary care providers (PCPs) and employed physicians' high patient expectations, including "sensationalized" Internet searches.

Some of this can be solved at the institutional level by having the hospital leadership insist that the culture be respectful of all health professionals, including physicians. The way that administrative leadership behaves and treats people will have a trickle-down effect.

Healthcare administrators as employers of physicians have a great opportunity to treat these professional employees as professionals. It is also necessary to treat nurses and all healthcare professionals that way, but I think one of the main differentiators is that physicians are new to the employee ranks. Many did not understand exactly what they bought into when they signed up. Expectations were that the hospital would ease all of their administrative burdens and let them practice medicine. This misunderstanding needs to be clarified. It will be highly dependent on managing the organizational culture – by no means a simple task.

Professionalism is also an issue with nursing. Organized nursing has been trying for many years to look at this. Advanced practice providers or nurse practitioners/physician assistants seem to have an even more significant issue. Each state's laws handle these providers' licensing and privileging differently, and their professional space is often in flux.

Another piece of this equation is helping the physicians identify their particular passion. Physicians need enough flexibility to focus on the things they really like to do; from a professional standpoint, this can be highly engaging. Perhaps it is a certain disease or a certain type of patient, but taking the time to understand this and allowing the physician to put some of their time into these areas will increase satisfaction dramatically.[12] It is important that physicians try to regain the meaning of what brought them into medicine in the first place.[13]

Team leadership is another important aspect of burnout prevention. Physicians are not typically trained as leaders, and, in fact, much of the training encourages them to be individualistic. Leadership training and having physician leadership models in the hospital outpatient setting can go a long way toward engaging physicians as leaders working with peers. Even physicians who are not formal leaders would benefit from some leadership in team-based training. This will also go a long way toward helping to prevent burnout.[12]

Some of this might include encouraging physicians and providing access to physician professional development activities. These can be clinical as well as nonclinical. Burnout training and awareness is also a piece of this.

Onboarding

Onboarding fits into a number of different categories, including professionalism, sense of community, creating efficiency, professionalism, and transparency. A robust onboarding process helps the new physician understand the organization, become part of the culture, and become integrated more quickly. There is a didactic portion of this which includes educating the physician on where to find things and how to get things done. Also it is helpful to assign a mentor to the new physician as an internal resource. This gives the person a link to the organization on an ongoing basis. While it is not within the scope of this book to go into the details of the onboarding processes, this can be a critical piece in getting physicians and healthcare workers integrated into the organization quickly and keeping them in the organization. It has been shown that a good onboarding process is a critical piece to creating the right culture.[11]

Disruptive Behavior

Disruptive behavior can be a real problem in a healthcare organization. It is also called "lateral or horizontal" violence, or workplace bullying. It can be very obvious such as surgeons throwing scalpels in the OR, or it can be very subtle such as whispers and innuendo. Both types of disruptive behavior can damage a culture. This can affect the mental health of staff and create a culture of disrespect that can make patient injury more likely.[14]

This is a cultural and tolerance issue, and one must have an open culture with free communication and have a zero tolerance policy for disruptive behavior. This can be very subtle so one must be acutely aware of its challenges.

Sense of Community

In the old days, physicians had a connection to the professional community both at the hospital and outside of the hospital. In the hospital, everyone would make rounds in the morning and there would be a chance to chat with each other, discuss patient care and other collegial issues. In addition, there was a physicians' lounge where most of the physicians would gather early in the morning. In the age of hospitalists, employed physicians, and specialist hospitalists, the hospitals are not necessarily centric to physicians' practices. There is little opportunity to chat with one's peers on a day-to-day basis.

Another source of this collegiality was the medical society. There were a number of social as well as patient-directed events that were often supported and managed by the local medical society. Medical societies, one might argue, have become much less a part of the typical physician's life.

Some substitutes to give physicians the chance to have meaningful dialogues with each other are new groups that are forming after hours. Physicians are getting together in small groups at the hospital, at a physician's house, or at a local restaurant to talk about some of their common goals, issues, and concerns. This is proving to be very beneficial to helping to share the burnout burden.[15]

Physicians as Employees

While physicians are becoming employees of large healthcare systems that add value to them, it can still affect their independence and professionalism. Physicians as a group are not used to being employees, and hospitals have consistently struggled on how to deal with "professional" employees.

This employment of physicians dramatically changes the dynamics from independent practitioners running a small mom-and-pop practice to dealing with large administrative departments, such as human resources (HR), legal, and other departments. Often there is no easy way to drive change from the bottom in these practices, and the individualism of physician styles and practices are hard to manage. There are several advantages, including paid time off, professional practice management, and financing an EMR system. Obviously, there are also many trade-offs.

In the past, when large entities tried to employ physicians, they were not successful. Keeping physicians engaged and allowing them enough autonomy to practice medicine with their individual styles, yet still maintain a level of practice consistency will be an ongoing challenge.

Fairness and Equitable Treatment

Virtually everyone responds positively to what they perceive as fairness and equitable treatment, so there is no reason to think it would be different with physicians or other medical personnel. Traditionally, there has been much inequity at the hospital and practice levels. This includes the different specialties of physicians as well as the newer challenge of nurse practitioners and physician assistants. Often the *perception* of fairness and equitable treatment is even more important than the reality. Hospitals in this new role as employer need to be sensitive to these issues.[16]

Transparency

It almost goes without saying that transparency is critical to a trusting and engaged relationship. Transparency transcends the entire healthcare arena. It is critical that there is transparency between the hospital as an employer, and physicians as employees. I would also advocate for transparency between payers and physicians.

There is generally a lack of trust between the hospital and physicians. This has been a long-standing issue and is better in some places and worse in others. The old adage of "physicians are from Venus and administrators are from Mars" has been kicking around for many years. Often physicians and nurses believe there is an anti-physician conspiracy behind closed c-suite doors at the hospital. This is rarely the case. It is critical that administrators be transparent with their strategies and financials to physicians on a consistent basis in a way that creates trust. This transparency can go a long way to helping alignment between hospitals and physicians. There are obviously other areas of transparency at the patient level that are important, but we will not get into them here.

Patient Relationships and Second Victim Syndrome

One of the most rewarding things in a medical practice for most physicians is the relationship with their patients. This has become more difficult in the fractured world of healthcare delivery. We now have PCPs who do not go to the hospital, hospitalists who do not go outside of the hospital, and intensivists who do not go outside of the ICU. This makes patient relationships more challenging and the communication process more difficult. It is important for a healthcare system and/or outpatient practice to make sure that patient/physician time is protected and made to be as meaningful as possible. This is about scheduling as well as EMR optimization and other office flow issues.

Physicians and other healthcare professionals are all susceptible to compassion fatigue and the "second victim syndrome." If any of the caregivers are involved in an unanticipated outcome, it can have a huge emotional impact on the physician or healthcare provider. It has been shown that the healthcare provider's blood pressure goes up, heart rate increases, muscle tension increases, and breathing increases. Difficulty in concentrating, poor appetite, and sleep disturbances are all part of this second victim syndrome. Healthcare providers who are suffering from it experience a range of emotions, including sadness, fear, guilt, anger, and humiliation. This can last from days to months and it is exacerbated by a physician's baseline mental state, especially burnout.[14]

Efficiency Inpatient/Outpatient

Minimizing administrative bottlenecks is probably one of the most important things to lessen burnout. It encompasses all of the other things in combination. This is about removing all the barriers to patient care. This is about minimizing all of the administrative and nonclinical tasks to allow physicians to spend time directly with their patients. The focus should be on improving care. This also applies to nonphysicians in minimizing the "task lists" that are part of most EMR's. We need to allow medical professionals to be at the bedside taking care of patients. In most cases physicians are the "bottlenecks" of the system and, as such, anything that can be used to mitigate this rate-limiting step should be undertaken.

This includes optimizing EMRs, minimizing time inputting information, and limiting the time it takes to obtain supplies. The amount of walking that healthcare professionals do in the hospital amounts to miles and miles. Looking at automating and developing protocols for as many nonclinical things as possible should be a priority.

In the inpatient setting, turnaround times (lab and radiology), intelligent alert settings, inefficient setup of procedures, and transportation processes all can lead to inefficiencies.

In the outpatient setting, or practice setting, many of the same things mentioned earlier apply. These include things such as optimizing EMRs, optimizing templates, office procedures that let staff practice at the top of their licenses, appropriate scheduling, and any other factor that leads to a more collegial and friendly office setting.

In this regard, moving toward a team-based care model and/or a patient-centered medical home model (PCMH) also affects the practice, making it less chaotic, less stressful, more productive, and thereby mitigating burnout.[17]

Communication

Communication is another large category with many opportunities. This includes communication from the hospital to physicians, physicians to physicians, and patients to physicians (and vice versa). Communication serves several purposes. One is to provide great care by getting the right information to the right place. The other important consideration is transparency, communication to engender engagement by the medical staff in the workings of the hospitals, and outpatient practices that medical staff are dependent on.

Allowing and encouraging physicians to meet in small groups has clearly been shown to help physicians deal with the stress and complexity of providing healthcare. These are often semi-structured, private discussions in restaurants and participants' homes that help to alleviate some of the social isolation that can be part of burnout.[9] Sometimes these groups can take on the form of what is called Balint groups. This is a group of clinicians who meet regularly to present clinical cases in order to improve and better understand the clinical/patient relationship.[14]

Training physicians to improve patient communication not only increases quality of care but also enhances the experience for both the physician and the patient. This has been proven to lead to less physician burnout.[18]

Dealing with Malpractice Crises

I believe the malpractice issue has been grossly undervalued in both healthcare costs and provider burnout. It has been clearly shown that burnout increases the malpractice risk, and also that the reverse is true: a malpractice experience accelerates burnout[19, 20] The stress and frustration of dealing with malpractice litigation cannot be overestimated.

Mental Health Support

It has always been challenging and difficult for physicians and other healthcare workers to ask for help. This is particularly true in the area of mental health. Making the services available in a nonjudgmental way is critical. We must make access easy, but also remove the stigma of accessing mental health treatment.

The other aspect of this in the healthcare and physician's world is that mental health is one of those things that is part of almost every application for medical staff privileges and/or payer contracts. This gives seeking care a direct impact on one's career or one's ability to achieve staff privileges. Something must be done to put a process in place to protect patients, but also to protect healthcare workers.

Creating a Wellness Committee and a Wellness Champion (Chief Wellness Officer)

It is important to focus not just on eliminating or mitigating burnout, but also to focus on wellness and health. This includes moving past the burnout issues and trying to create physician and healthcare worker engagement and wellness. We are seeing many large organizations that are actually hiring a chief wellness officer as a point person to focus on both the burnout initiatives but also on moving the organizational culture to health and wellness. It is important to try to bring joy back into the practice of healthcare[21] (Figure 7.2.).

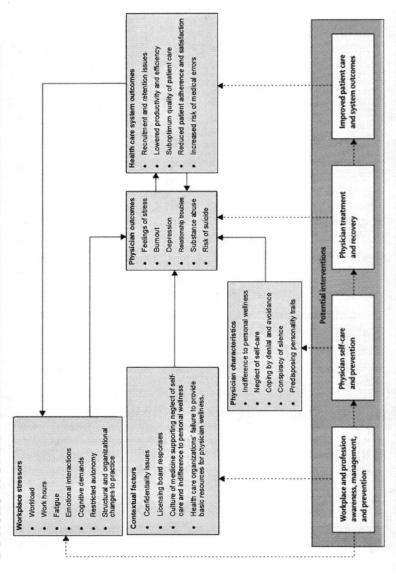

Figure 7.2 Physicians path to wellness. Used with permission; Eschelbach, MM, (November 2018), A Proposed Review and Fix for Physician Burnout, Physician Leaders. Retrieved from: https://www.physicianleaders.org/news/proposed-review-fix-physician-burnout

Changing the Culture

There is no one easy solution to burnout. It is about multiple small solutions that will ultimately mitigate these issues. It is easy to see that the solutions are often systemic across the organization, but also cross over onto the individual.

The ultimate goal of any healthcare organization should be to create a great place to work with happy employees and a patient-focused environment. Many studies have shown that when employees are happy and engaged, the patient experience and outcome are better. All of these items contribute to an improved culture. This cannot be managed with multiple projects focused on preventing burnout; it must focus on preventing burnout as a cultural issue. Equally important, we must focus on a culture of wellness, engagement, and satisfaction. It would be nice if in the future we are able to shift from measuring burnout to measuring "happiness" and engagement (Figure 7.2).

Transition to Value-Based Care

I am cautiously optimistic that as we transition to value-based care that some of the solutions mentioned will become necessary as part of this transition. Value-based care shifts the responsibility of cost, quality, outcomes, and patient experience to the delivery system. The big game changer here is the responsibility for costs. Accountability and rewarding outcomes, and not only rewarding processes, should help physicians focus on what is right for patients and be able to balance resource utilization with outcomes and costs. Only clinicians can do this. This should set the stage for aligned financial incentives and facilitate leadership, transparency, and an efficient and effective healthcare model.

Solutions List for Improving Organization Burnout

Work hours and time off: Work/life balance[22]

- Ensure workload expectations are reasonable
- Align financial incentives appropriately
- Give physicians some autonomy and control over their work hours
- Clarify job duties and responsibilities
- Give control physicians more control over their schedules and allow flexibility
- Respect home boundaries and home priorities
- Develop a reasonable call schedule with time to catch up on sleep

Improving workflow

- Schedule patients for the appropriate amount of time
- Create a culture of team-based approach
- Focus on workflow to automate as many processes as possible
- Address hospital-wide
- Create committees focusing on patient flow

Electronic Medical Records

- Give physicians a choice on how they will enter data (e.g. scribes)
- Maximize office staff to help input EMR information
- Restructure alerts and in-basket to minimize alert fatigue
- Provide regular EHR training and encourage superuser status
- Maximize macros/templates and other efficiency steps
- Work with chief medical information officer to maximize EHR usage

Changing the culture

- Encourage physician leadership and engagement
- Focus on the professional culture
- Remain intolerant to disruptive behavior
- Create a robust onboarding process
- Foster a sense of community
- Encourage fairness, and transparency
- Provide access to mental health resources in a nonjudgmental way
- Communicate, communicate, communicate
- Focus on wellness and health

Bibliography

1. Berg, S. (2017, November 2). To address burnout's underlying causes, look to team-based care. Retrieved from https://www.ama-assn.org/practice-management/physician-health/address-burnouts-underlying-causes-look-team-based-care.
2. Henry, Tonya Albert (2019, July 5). Burnout's mounting price tag: What it's costing your organization, American Medical Association. Retrieved from https://www.ama-assn.org/practice-management/physician-health/burnout-s-mounting-price-tag-what-it-s-costing-your.
3. Berg, Sara (2018, October 11). How much physicians' burnout is costing your organization, American Medical Association. Retrieved from: https://www.ama-assn.org/practice-management/economics/how-much-physician-burnout-costing-your-organization.
4. Shanafeldt, T., Goh, J., & Sinsky, C. (2017, September). The business case for investing in physician well-being. *JAMA Internal Medicine, 2017*, 4340.
5. Stone, M. (2017, November 10). Fighting physician burnout at the organizational level. Retrieved from https://news.physicianleaders.org/fighting-physician-burnout-at-the-organizational-level.
6. Opinion: It's time to treat physician burnout's root causes. (2018, January 5). Retrieved from https://labblog.uofmhealth.org/industry-dx/opinion-its-time-to-treat-physician-burnouts-root-causes.

7. Berg, Sara (2017, September 11). Family doctor spent 86 minutes of "pajama time" with e HR's nightly, American Medical Association. Retrieved from https://www.ama-assn.org/practice-management/digital/family-doctors-spend-86-minutes-pajama-time-ehrs-nightly.
8. Kevi, M.D., anonymous. (2019, May 25). It's time for physicians to be less "productive." Retrieved from https://www.kevinmd.com/blog/2019/05/its-time-for-physicians-to-be-less-productive.html.
9. Jerzak, J. (2017, May/June) Radical design: The power of team base care. *The Annals of Family Medicine, 15*(3), 281. Retrieved from http://www.annfammed.org/content/15/3/281.full.
10. Fassiotto, M.A. Stanford University school of medicine, time banking system to support workplace flexibility. Retrieved from http://wellmd.stanford.edu/content/dam/sm/wellmd/documents/Time-banking-system.pdf.
11. Berg, S. (2017, September) Burned out? You're not alone. Here's how two doctors overcame it, AMA. Retrieved from https://www.ama-assn.org/practice-management/physician-health/burned-out-you-re-not-alone-here-s-how-2-doctors-overcame-it.
12. Schuite, B. (2015, August). Time in the bank: Hey Stanford plan to save doctors from burnout. *Washington Post*. Retrieved from https://www.washingtonpost.com/news/inspired-life/wp/2015/08/20/the-innovative-stanford-program-thats-saving-emergency-room-doctors-from-burnout/.
13. Kimmel, Jackie (2018, October 30). The five biggest risk factors for physician burnout, according to our 13,371 – physician survey. Advisory board. Retrieved from https://www.advisory.com/daily-briefing/2018/10/30/burnout.
14. Berg, S. https://www.ama-assn.org/practice-management/physician-health/leadership-development-may-be-linked-reduced-burnout-rates.
15. Cheney, C. (2018, June 21). Two kinds of interventions reduce physician burnout. Retrieved from https://www.healthleadersmedia.com/clinical-care/two-kinds-interventions-reduce-physician-burnout.
16. Norcal Group. (2018, December). Systems solutions to decreasing physician burnout and increasing wellness. *Claims Rx*, 12–18 Retrieved from https://files.norcal-group.com/hubfs/Resources/NORCAL_ClaimsRx_Burnout-Wellness_12-18.pdf.

17. Berg, Sara. (2018, April 4). Four lessons Mayo Clinic learned from group meetings to cut burnout, American Medical Association. Retrieved from https://www.ama-assn.org/practice-management/physician-health/4-lessons-mayo-clinic-learned-group-meetings-cut-burnout.
18. Dechant, Paul. (2018, February 18). Absence of fairness and burnout. Retrieved from http://www.pauldechantmd.com/absence-of-fairness-burnout/.
19. Pena, Cindy. (2017, November 15). Insight healthcare: Reenergizing your practice – How the PCM a smile impacts physician burnout, and secure a blog. Retrieved from https://blog.ncqa.org/re-energizing-your-practice-how-the-pcmh-model-impacts-physician-burnout/.
20. Berg, Sara (2017, July 7), Better communication with patients linked to less burnout, American Medical Association. Retrieved from https://www.ama-assn.org/practice-management/physician-health/better-communication-patients-linked-less-burnout.
21. Kopynec, Suze (2019, May 1). Provider burnout and the risk of malpractice, a APA news. Retrieved from https://www.aapa.org/news-central/2018/05/provider-burnout-and-the-risk-of-malpractice/.
22. Becker's Hospital News. (2011, November 15). Malpractice lawsuits linked to physician burnout, dissatisfaction. Retrieved from https://www.beckershospitalreview.com/news-analysis/malpractice-lawsuits-linked-to-physician-burnout-dissatisfaction.html.
23. Kishore, Sandeep, Ripp, Jonathan, Shanafelt, T. et al. (2018, October 26) Making the case for the chief wellness officer in America's health systems: A call to action. *Health Affairs*. Retrieved from https://www.healthaffairs.org/do/10.1377/hblog20181025.308059/full/.
24. Cheney, Christopher. (2018, June 21). Two kinds of interventions reduce physician burnout, Health leaders. Retrieved from https://www.healthleadersmedia.com/clinical-care/two-kinds-interventions-reduce-physician-burnout.
25. DrummondD. (n.d.). *Physician Burnout: Why It's Not a Fair Fight*. Retrieved from https://www.thehappymd.com/blog/bid/295048/Physician-Burnout-Why-its-not-a-Fair-Fight.

26. Drummond, D. (n.d.). *Physician Burnout - The Three Symptoms, Three Phases and Three Cures.* Retrieved from https://www.thehappymd.com/blog/bid/290755/physician-burnout-the-three-symptoms-three-phases-and-three-cures.
27. Fry, E., & Schulte, F. (2019, March 18). *Death by a Thousand Clicks: Where Electronic Health Records Went Wrong.* Retrieved from https://fortune.com/longform/medical-records/.
28. Goodman, M. & Berlinerblau, M. (2018, January 5). Discussion: Treating burnout by addressing its causes. Retrieved from https://news.physicianleaders.org/discussion-treating-burnout-by-addressing-its-causes.
29. Hockman, D.E. (2018, May 15). *A Relatively Simple Solution to Physician Burnout.* Retrieved from https://www.kevinmd.com/blog/2018/05/a-relatively-simple-solution-to-physician-burnout.html.
30. Jain, S.H. (2018, December 21). *One Solution to Physician Burnout: Appreciation.* Retrieved from https://www.forbes.com/sites/sachinjain/2018/12/21/more-gratitude-one-solution-to-address-the-looming-crisis-of-physician-burnout/#5e7e4ec484d4.
31. Kalani, S.D., Azadfallah, P., Oreyzi, H., & Adibi, P. (2018). Interventions for physician burnout: A systematic review. *International Journal of Preventive Medicine, 9*, 81.
32. Kumar, R. (n.d.). *5 Ways to Reduce Physician Burnout Caused by EHRs.* Retrieved from https://www.softwareadvice.com/resources/reduce-physician-burnout/.
33. Maslach, S., Jackson, S.E., Leiter, M.P., Schaufeli, W.B. & Schwab, R.L. *Maslach Burnout Toolkit.* Retrieved from https://www.mindgarden.com/184-maslach-burnout-toolkit.
34. Montanez, R. (2018, March 5). *Powerful Solutions to Help Stop and Prevent Burnout.* Retrieved from https://www.forbes.com/sites/ellevate/2018/03/05/powerful-solutions-to-help-stop-and-prevent-burnout/#176330163a47.
35. Physician burnout solutions. (n.d.). Retrieved from https://www.mindgarden.com/content/34-physician-burnout-solutions.
36. Reducing physician burnout. (2016, June 1). Retrieved from https://www.hopkinsmedicine.org/office-of-johns-hopkins-physicians/best-practice-news/reducing-physician-burnout.
37. West, C.P., Dyrbye, L.N., & Shanafelt, T.D. (2018). Physician burnout: Contributors, consequences and solutions. *The Association for the Publication of the Journal of Internal Medicine, 283*(6), 516–529.

Chapter 8

The Disillusioned Physician and the Electronic Medical Record

George Mayzell

Contents

One of the most important contributors to burnout is the electronic medical record (EMR). In March 2017, 67% of all providers reported using an electronic health record (EHR), and as of 2015 about 87% of office-based physicians had adopted an EHR. Since 2008, physician office adoption rates have nearly doubled. It should be noted that nearly 40% of hospital executives are either indifferent to or dissatisfied with the current EHR system.[1]

Conventional wisdom would indicate that the electronic medical record and physician burnout go hand in hand. Although most would agree that the medical record is a large contributor to burnout, there is more to the story.

It was becoming clear that outcomes and communication in healthcare were not where they needed to be, that cost and quality measurement was imperative, and that development of a comprehensive EMR strategy was critical. Unfortunately, the integration of physician and healthcare workers' workflow was not prioritized. In fact, one of the biggest issues in the EMR's evolution is the fact that clinicians were not intimately involved in the initial development. In a study they conducted in 2006, Merritt and Hawkins found that only 11% of physicians reported that they felt the EHR had improved patient interactions, compared to 60% who said it had made these interactions worse.[2,3]

There is significant evidence that the EMR has had a huge impact on physician workflow, time constraints, and burnout. We replaced paper with computers to gain efficiency, and now we're having to hire more people (scribes and others) to support this new system. Some examples of its challenging impact are:

- Emergency room physicians average 4,000 total mouse clicks for charting and documenting patient encounters during a 10-hour shift.[2,3]
- EMR documentation requires 6.5 hours more per week than a paper record system.[2,3]
- EMR use reduces productivity by 20% to 40%.[2,3]
- For every patient seen in the office, a physician receives a non-visit-related inbox message for another four patients.[4]

The Journey to the EMR

In 1999 the Institute of Medicine published an article entitled "To Err Is Human." In this article they noted that as many as 98,000 people die each year from medical errors in hospitals.[5] This article helped to change the thinking about how safe hospitals were, and should be. In this article it was noted that these deaths surpassed many other causes of common fatalities including motor vehicle accidents, cancers, and AIDS.

There were follow-ups to this article in 2010 and 2014 entitled "Mirror, Mirror on the Wall." These follow up publications, published by the Commonwealth Fund, noted that the United States was still struggling with healthcare quality and outcomes and noted significant underperformance relative to other countries on many dimensions.[6,7]

It was frustrating to all that, even with a 15-year gap between these articles, accomplishments and progress were unimpressive in providing a safer healthcare environment.

There were many recommendations that came out of these revelations. One of these was a clear need for an electronic medical record complete with interoperability and easy access to medical information for both patients and physicians.

In 2009 the HITECH Act (Health Information Technology for Economic and Clinical Health Act) helped to change the current landscape of healthcare delivery. This was an expansive legislation that was created to expand electronic medical record use and adoption and to help provide financial support to encourage this.[8]

These incentive dollars were designed to cover the purchase and investment required to bring EMRs into hospitals and clinics. It was hoped this would increase communication, decrease medical errors, and provide better healthcare outcomes.

The government offered billions of dollars to correct a system without a fully elucidated strategy. Initially the healthcare industry resisted this change; however, the stimulus with all its economic incentives brought a number of new players and multiple initiatives to the marketplace. The price and fees for noncompliance were also a small factor; however, there was a large incentive to bring EMRs into the hospital and outpatient setting.

This stimulus package created an approximately a $35 billion[9] opportunity to create something that would help healthcare providers document care. These tools were a great opportunity for newly founded EMR companies to make money and allow physicians and hospitals to comply with these meaningful use standards and receive significant financial incentives. The challenge was that the time for marketing and implementation was very brief, causing vendors to move into the market without being fully prepared. There were several inadequate systems that were put in the hands of providers.

Often these early EMRs were designed and built by nonclinical people. The focus was to capture appropriate clinical information to bill insurance companies and Medicare for services. The systems were often cumbersome. Without physicians and clinical leaders helping to design the workflow, they were often clunky and inadequate for hospital or office use. It would've been critical for physicians and clinical leaders to take a more active role in the EMR development and build; however, for various reasons this did not occur.

Fortunately, this situation is slowly changing. EMRs are now being adopted with significant clinical input to mirror the workflow of clinicians. More hospitals and health systems are hiring chief medical information officers (CMIOs) to help assist in these processes. Most of the top software vendors are now optimizing their EMRs moving toward interoperability with a focus on having a more patient- and physician-centric approach.

EMR Issues and Burnout

In a recent article in JAMA,[10] there was a description of the most common causes of physician burnout as it relates to the work conditions put forth by the EHR. The findings revealed that excessive data entry, note bloat, notes focused on billing, fear of missing information, the complexities of navigating the system, slow response times, information overload, and interference in the patient-clinician relationship as the most common causes of frustration with the EMR. Pain and posture problems related to prolonged sitting at the keyboard were also noted (Figure 8.1).

Information Overload

One of the most substantial elements contributing to burnout comes from information overload. An example of this is that physicians try to incorporate all sorts of data elements from other EMRs, labs, radiology, and others into the medical record. In the past, a good medical record captured the relevant items without a lot of the nonrelevant items. Now medical records can be long and redundant. Often the easiest thing to do is to cut and paste from the prior day's note. This can result in inaccurate information and/or multipage documents, making it hard to locate relevant findings. The EMR software has "created the massive monster of incomprehensibility," said Dr. Sadoughi.[11]

From an outside perspective, the advancement of the EMR was seen as a boon to the industry, but from the perspective

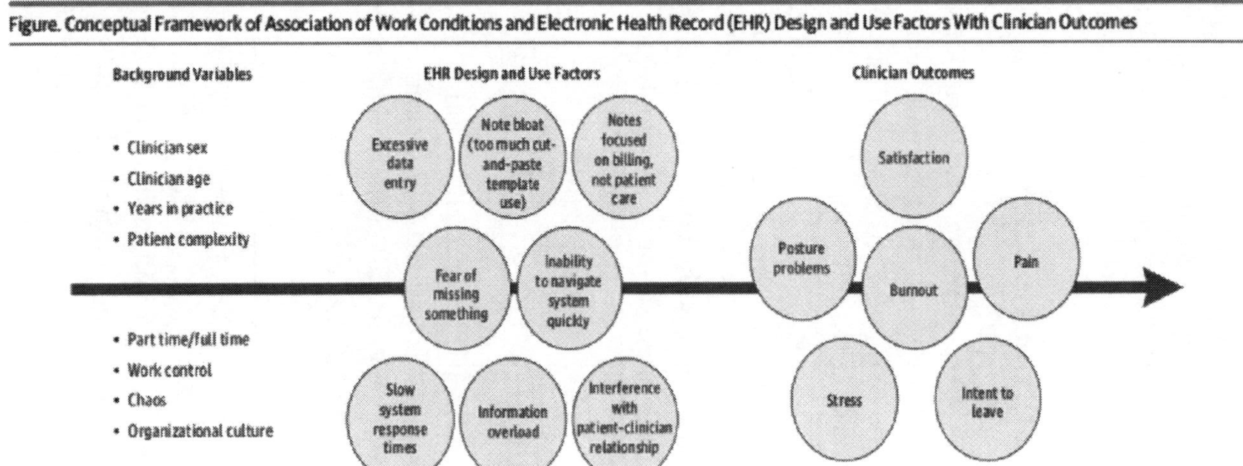

Figure 8.1 Challenges with the EMR. (Kroth, P.J., Morioka-Douglas, N.M., Veres, S., et al. (2019) Association of electronic health record design and use factors with clinician stress and burnout. *JAMA Network Open*, 2(8), e199609. doi:10.1001/jamanetworkopen.2019.9609.)

of a clinician trying to get through a busy day, this information overload is insurmountable. Sadly, this data, much of which is not relevant, takes a tremendous amount of time to go through, and providers are aware there is tremendous legal liability if they miss something that may be deeply buried in the electronic record.

Another Factor of Information Overload – Alert Fatigue

Because of the complexity of healthcare information and the mountain of data, there is a potential for the EMRs to identify critical issues and alert providers to potential dangers. These "alerts" can come in the form of drug–drug, drug–disease, and drug–dose interactions as well as a host of other areas. These can be lifesaving, allowing providers the opportunity to change orders or initiate care plan changes. The challenge is identifying which alerts are critical and which alerts are not important. According to one study, there were 64.1 passive alerts/patient per day of which only 4.5% were for panic values.[13] There have been numerous studies showing that although these practice alerts contribute to improving patient care, there are also studies that show that alert fatigue can risk physicians and others missing important information.

Data Entry Is Hard

In the old days of paper charts, physician documentation was minimal and was often only minimally acceptable. At that time, notes were hard to read, orders were complicated, and notes did not follow any standard process. Errors were common. In order to fix this issue, the legislature and electronic records companies, along with other mandates (risk, compliance, etc.), instituted computerized physician order entry (CPOE). This process has the physicians directly place all orders into the computer. In the past, orders were written by physicians or given verbally, and an assistant would log them into the system. This led to translation errors from illegible orders as well as other issues.

On the surface, this concept makes perfect sense. By having clinicians place their own orders, and do so in a standardized fashion, errors should be minimized, patient outcomes should improve, and less harm would come to patients. Sadly, however, this approach came with unintended consequences. Along with appropriate data entry for orders come the need for indications for imaging, best practice advisories, coding query requirements, and billing requirements. In some institutions, there is an overall sense that if physicians do not enter the information themselves, the data point is not accurate. Each additional piece of information in and of itself is typically small; however, when you add them all together, they are quite cumbersome.

This may not seem like a large undertaking, but some studies have shown that doctors now spend about two hours on documentation for every hour they devote to patient care. While there are certain "tricks of the trade" that a "superuser" can master, it is still quite challenging to get all of the appropriate information into the EMR.

Many of the solutions have been centered on outsourcing these clerical functions, which adds cost and complexity to an already overburdened process. These outsourcing solutions include medical scribes and virtual scribes who do the medical record documentation at the direction of the physician. Virtual scribes are the newest solution. These companies are able to listen to the physician-patient visit from offsite (with permission) while a virtual scribe employed medical students or other medically oriented employees (some outside of the country) put together an appropriate progress note, which is then approved by the healthcare provider.[13] I am sure that there will be many more of these disruptors in the future. In 2015, a study of scribes found a 36% reduction in the doctors' computer-documentation time and a similar increase in time spent with patients.[11]

In the exam room, physicians spend half of their time facing the computer screen.[11] To improve their efficiency, providers must focus not on clinical acumen, but also on becoming an EMR expert, putting in macros or templates, saving preferences, building notes, and setting up personal order sets. None of these put the patient in the center of the healthcare experience. The issue is so pervasive that Dr. Mark Friedberg has been noted to say in a mock voice, "I once saw a doctor make eye contact with the patient. The horror must stop."[8]

According to the Mayo Clinic, one of the strongest predictors of burnout was how much time each individual spent doing computer documentation, including the time spent at home working on documentation.[11] The EMR which was originally pitched as a work enhancer has proven to be one of the greatest physician stressors leading to burnout.

Errors

EMRs have the potential to be much safer than their paper counterparts. They can ferret out drug-drug interactions, focus our attention on allergies, and include best practice advisories. Unfortunately, they also have the potential for errors at the user level. Drug selection and drug-dosing issues are a common cause of errors in the EMR. When you consider, for example, the vast number of formulations of morphine, Tylenol, and heparin, it is easy to see how incorrect dosing, formulations, or delivery routes could be selected inadvertently.

Quantros, a healthcare analytics firm, said that they logged 18,000 EHR-related safety events from 2007 to 2018, 3% of which resulted in patient harm, including seven deaths.[14]

One example: To order Tylenol there was a drop-down menu with one EHR having 86 different listing options. Many were irrelevant for a particular patient. Physicians had to read the list carefully so as not to click the wrong dosage form. In roughly one out of a thousand orders, physicians accidentally selected the suppository form by accident. While this was not a safety issue, I'm sure the patients were less than thrilled with getting a rectal dose of medicine they should have gotten orally.[14]

In 2016, in a test simulation, the Leapfrog Group noted that EHRs failed to flag potential harmful drug orders in 39% of cases. In 13% of those cases, the mistake could have been fatal.[14]

We are all looking forward to some of the benefits of the EMR. According to Meyer, we are only beginning to get some of these benefits. Researchers looked at Medicare patients admitted to hospitals for 15 common conditions and analyzed their 30-day death rates. In the first years of the EMR, death rates actually increased; however, after that the deaths dropped 21% a year for every function added. This has tremendous long-term potential for patient safety.[11]

The Problem List is Really a Problem

The problem list is supposed to be a list of diagnoses and issues that each doctor can peruse as a reference to see what problems are active, or historical. This has not worked out as planned. There are a number of technical issues and also workflow issues. First the technical issues.

The ICD 10 code set (International Classification of Diseases) which was recently adopted, has nearly 68,000 codes.[15] It was meant to capture detailed patient specific diagnoses. Unfortunately, there are so many codes that the only way to deal with it is through electronic means. There are two major technical problems. The first is that there are so many codes that are superfluous and don't really add any value. These include codes such as:[16]

T Z63.1 – Problems in relationship with in-laws.
W61.43 – Pecked by a turkey.
W22.02 – Walked into lamppost.
W97.33 – Sucked into a jet engine.

There are also many codes which are similar and overlap, creating increasing confusion when trying to code for a single disease. As an example, there are 95[17] different codes for acute congestive heart failure. These overlap and often don't differentiate clinically in any way. This makes it likely that individual physicians while coding for the same disease may use different codes.

Even if we can get past all of the technical issues, one of the major issues is in the clinical workflow. There is frequently no one in charge of the problem list. Each time a physician goes into the chart and creates a diagnosis this automatically updates the problem list, creating duplications and confusing issues between active problems, old problems and rule out problems. Everyone is in charge, so no one's in charge. This makes the problem list often unusable. Unless physicians can all agree on how the problem list will be managed, and can make sure that it is current and that the EMR does not add "noise," it will remain little used.

Note Bloat

Similar to the information overload problem is the problem of "note bloat." There are too many things dragged into the note and there is too much "copy and paste." There are detailed templates to assist in documentation as well as dashboards that show all sorts of pertinent information that can be viewed alongside the note. These are all often underused. These should mitigate the need to copy and drag in all sorts of information into the daily note. Nonetheless, physicians continue to bring loads of detail into their notes.

To take it a step further, some physicians copy nearly every note to the primary care physician, placing that note in the provider's in-basket. This occurs despite the fact that every note is easily available electronically and may not need to be shared daily.

There is pending Centers for Medicare and Medicaid Services (CMS) regulation that is being drafted to standardize billing. That plan will remove levels of billing, and CMS will allow only one level for a fee schedule. With this, the note requirements will change dramatically. The rationale for this is to minimize the work effort and complexities in the payment structure from a payer perspective. This plan implementation is now delayed.[18]

Work Conditions and the EMR

Another impactful finding is the effects of poor EMR infrastructure. Specifically, slow EMR response times are extremely frustrating. It would be nice and easy to say that there is no excuse for this in 2019, given our current technology. However, the truth of the matter is that many of our hospitals were built many years ago and are aging.

The physical infrastructure of the hospital itself stands in the way of the electronic infrastructure. To mitigate slow response times, information technology (IT) departments all around the country optimize Wi-Fi signal repeaters and every sort of gadget, but the infrastructure and types of construction of older buildings often interfere with these Wi-Fi signals. The ongoing demand for increasing bandwidth as required by electronic radiology images, dictation systems enabled by Wi-Fi, and other large-format electronic transmissions continue to challenge infrastructure.

There is continued demand for interfaces, interactivity, HIPPA Compliant texting, and other complicated electronic information that requires data to flow effortlessly into the physicians' and healthcare workers' hands in a timely and responsive fashion. Sadly, there is often a suboptimal experience because of infrastructure limitations.

Cut and Paste

Cut and paste is on the same genre as note bloat. This is the scenario in which a clinician may copy his/her own notes (or someone else's) from yesterday and paste them into today's daily note. Many providers in leadership view this as unacceptable. If done correctly, it may be a way for clinicians to save time and use EMRs to their advantage. Much of the time, the patient's physical exam, medical history, and surgical histories, are mostly unchanged. To re-create daily notes that are effectively unchanged each day is not necessarily efficient. Having said that, copying and pasting would not be an issue as long as that new note is updated and edited. The challenge is that often the notes are not completely updated, if areas are missed, this can lead to inaccurate information that often keeps being brought forward. Also, this can create consistent wordy notes that convey minimal real clinical information.

Physician Leadership

Hospitals should be places where providers are in an active leadership role and engage in operational work that improves hospital outcomes, quality, efficiency, and financial stewardship. This takes physician and non-physician partnerships.

For example, to clarify the problem list, it would be easy for each physician to add a problem based on his/her own specialty and then request that the hospitalists resolve conflicts. This would provide a clean problem list for all physicians, both inpatient and outpatient. It is up to the organization and physician leaders to work with physicians and assist them in problem solving.

Potential Solutions[19] Figure 8.2

- Provide sufficient EHR training
- Select an internal EHR champion
- Set an easy-to-follow training schedule
- Improve the HR login and password process
- Improve workflows
- Search and identify process improvements
- Leverage templates or other shortcuts
- Know your computer system inside and out
- Tap into live or virtual medical scribes
- Evaluate the resources and people needed to maintain the EHR
- Consider a specialty-specific EHR/interface

Spitzer, J. , (July 2018). Six stats on the HR related physician burnout and 7 tips to combat it, *Beckers Hospital Review*, Retrieved from https://www.beckershospitalreview.com/ehrs/6-stats-on-ehr-related-physician-burnout-and-7-tips-to-combat-it.html
Kumar R., (September 2018). Five ways to reduce physician burnout caused by EHR's, *Software advice*, retrieved from https://www.softwareadvice.com/resources/reduce-physician-burnout/

Figure 8.2 Ways to tame the EMR

Training, Training, Training

It is all about managing physician and medical staff workflow and getting the most value with the least administrative hassle out of each EMR. To do this, everyone must be trained to the maximum. This includes mandated training with the goal of moving everyone toward superuser expertise. There will, of course, be some resistance since this takes time away from the office. In the long run, however, it will add to efficiency and mitigate some of the frustration that comes with not understanding and using the full functionality of the EMR.

There must be set training and retraining schedules in which the goal is to learn the systems inside and out. This includes learning how to create templates and macros so that the office and hospital workflow can be the most efficient possible. An internal physician champion should be selected. The superusers and hospital experts need to be available when physicians and other staff are making rounds. Training is perhaps the most critical issue in mitigating some of the inefficiencies that come with EHRs, especially in the short run.

Easy Log On

The need for easy log should go without saying. It should be easy to log on and stay logged on during the entire rounding period. Balancing security risks against efficiency should always be a goal.

Single touch sign on is a necessity. Think about the challenge to either a physician or nurse who has to log onto the computer 30, 40, or 50 times a day on different patients to either enter or visualize orders, labs, and notes. The cumulative time spent on log can be significant. There also needs to be a simple process to log on from outside the office so that work can be done from anywhere quickly and easily.

It Is All About Workflow

The computer should fit into the physicians' and nurses' workflow and not the other way around. Time should be spent evaluating how things get done, and then the computer should be a tool that helps create efficiency in the current workflow. So, if step one needs to happen first, such as registration, this needs to be put into the computer as such. The complexity of the hospital processes can make this difficult since often steps need to be skipped or mitigated based on acute patient needs. Time should be spent to maximize computer systems to let physicians and nurses have more time to take care of patients. This is perhaps one of the biggest problems with the EMR since for the most part these were created as billing and administrative tools and not clinical tools. This makes them often inefficient in tracking and trending clinical information and in supplying clinical information to staff. Many of the EMR systems have created workarounds so that these tools are slowly becoming more clinically focused. This is where physician and nursing input is critical. They must be involved in the workflow process designs. One challenge is that each hospital or system customized their system their own way. This makes each system, even from the same manufacturer, very different.

As stated earlier, physicians spend about two hours on the computer for every hour they spend with the patient. Approximately 50% of their time is spent on the EMR while only 27% of their time is spent on direct contact with the patient.[4] Changes must be made to let the physicians spend more time interacting with patients.

In addition, many clicks have been added to the EMR to support compliance and administration needs. We must "get rid of the stupid stuff" according to Dr. Ashton. We have to cut out much of the unnecessary work that used to be done by ancillary staff or, in fact, may not need to be done at all. One more click is still one more click.[20] Fields that were often skipped in the past now are "field required" and, therefore, must be answered before one can go on to finish inputting information. This can cause significant bottlenecks.[19]

Messaging and alert management are also part of the workflow. Alert fatigue is a real problem. Doctors get more than 100 messages per week in their in-baskets. There must be an automated way of separating the important from the unimportant.[14] Additionally, according to a 2016 Medscape study, physicians received an average of 79.6 notifications a day and on average spend more than an hour responding to these EHR alerts each day.[21] Clinicians admitted to ignoring safety notifications between 49% and 96% of the time according to a Harvard Medical School study.[21]

There is no end in sight to improving workflow. We must continue to commit time, energy, money, and resources to continuously improve the workflow process and its integration with the EMR.

Everybody Working at the Top of Their License

It is inefficient for physicians and nurses to spend a lot of time inputting information into the EMR system. Until we have better dictation systems and/or better artificial intelligence (AI) systems to input information, we will still have to do much of it manually. One of the trends, as previously stated, is to use scribes and virtual scribes to help input data. This is an additional resource and not a long-term solution. In the interim, it mitigates time spent on data input.

Scribes do the inputting of data either at the hospital or at the physician's office. Virtual scribes work remotely with the scribe listening to the office visit with the patient's permission and inputting the data into the medical record with physician oversight from a remote location. Some of the sites are overseas. One in particular is a program in India that has medical students and other medical experts serving in this capacity.[22]

Resources, Resources, Resources

The criticality of the EMR system is becoming more apparent but so is its potential to bottleneck a hospital or practice. As hospitals (and offices) get savvier, resources need to be dedicated to helping workflow and updates. The CMIO is critical in the hospital, but resources need to be right sized so systems can continually be improved and updated.

Connectivity and Interfaces

This is one of the largest challenges. Often inpatient EMR systems do not connect adequately to outpatient EMR systems if they are from different manufacturers or even a different version from the same manufacturer. Medical information is not smoothly transitioned from inpatient to outpatient or from one outpatient system to another. The interfaces for lab, x-ray, and other departments are often incompatible. This is something that will have to be dealt with. Oftentimes information may be shared as a scanned or PDF format. This is better than not having it, but the information cannot be easily searched, or trended at the individual data point.

One of the goals of the HITECH Act was interoperability. Many healthcare providers have not gone far enough. They could not justify the fees required to interface their EHRs with other healthcare providers. Even though there are some penalties, many physicians have made the decision to incur the penalties rather than spend more money on their EHR systems. Often one of the major reasons for physicians to become employed with a hospital is to help finance the practice's EMR.

There are culture and financial challenges that make it difficult to connect; many of the vendors consider this creating a competitive disadvantage. In an issue called "information blocking," these healthcare vendors are accused of intentionally interfering with the flow of information to different EHR systems. Also, the cost of interfaces can be very high, and multiple interfaces are often needed with continuing updates as newer and different versions of the EMR software are brought to market.[1]

There are always new interfaces that are being developed to deal with this. To reach the full promise of the EMR, it will require true universal interfaces and connectivity.

Summary

In summary, the EMR is here to stay, but it cannot stay in its current form. The first steps are to maximize its use and usability through knowledge, templates, and eliminating unnecessary steps. In the future it is really about redesigning the system to allow for easier and faster inputs, easier and better access to information, and much more interoperability with linkages to other healthcare data. This will help to mitigate burnout.

It will be important to move away from only using discrete fields and allowing real language processing capabilities. To get the most of these EMRs, it is not just about data at the population level or data at the practice level; we must be able to provide better care to the patients on an individual basis through decision support and embedded knowledge inside the system. This will only work if the system becomes as easy to use as paper charts. There are clearly some interesting things in the future, including the use of AI to help handle some of these inefficiencies.

It would be great to see these EMRs actually be flexible enough to fit into individual or group physician workflows. Obviously, part of this solution is to have physicians be more consistent with the workflow process. It would be nice to see EMRs automatically pull up gaps in care both for preventive care and for chronic disease processes that would be integrated into the current medical record as the patient is being evaluated in the office. These queries must be built right into the patient flow process, making it easy for the physician to do the right thing and order preventive and chronic care tests. Additionally, it would be great to have the EMR help with decision-support, building updated and new medical information and evidence-based care processes directly into the EMR in a seamless and easy to navigate process. Any decision support or other information must be continually updated as new information becomes available.

Obviously integrating other sources of data such as wearables, virtual visits, direct patient input information, social media and social determinants of health into the EMR would help us move from healthcare delivery to "health" delivery.

If these EMRs can become tools to improve care and allow healthcare workers to become more efficient, then they can cease contributing to burnout and rise to their true potential.

Bibliography

1. EHR adoption rates: 20 must-see stats. (2017, March 1). *Practice Fusion*. Retrieved from https://www.practicefusion.com/blog/ehr-adoption-rates/.

2. Larson, J. (2018, September 11). *The Leading Cause of Physician Burnout, What You Can Do.* Retrieved from https://www.staffcare.com/the-leading-cause-of-physician-burnout/;
3. Beresford, L. (2016, April). *Research Shows Link Between EHR and Physician Burnout.* Retrieved from https://www.the-hospitalist.org/hospitalist/article/121721/research-shows-link-between-ehr-and-physician-burnout.
4. Marcus, H. (2018). *Physician Burnout: Defining the Problems, Revealing the Solutions.* Retrieved from https://www.thedoctors.com/the-doctors-advocate/second-quarter-2018/Physician-Burnout-Defining-the-Problems-Revealing-the-Solutions/.
5. Institute of medicine, to err is human: Building a safer health system. (1999, November). Retrieved from http://www.nationalacademies.org/hmd/~/media/Files/Report%20Files/1999/To-Err-is-Human/To%20Err%20is%20Human%201999%20%20report%20brief.pdf.
6. Davis, K, Schoen, C, & Stremkis, K. (2010, June). Mirror, mirror on the wall: How the performance of the US healthcare system compares internationally, 2010 update. Retrieved from https://www.commonwealthfund.org/publications/fund-reports/2010/jun/mirror-mirror-wall-how-performance-us-health-care-system.
7. Davis, K., Stremikis, K., Squires, D., & Schoen, C. (2014). Mirror mirror on the wall, 2014 update; how the US health care system compares internationally. Retrieved from https://www.commonwealthfund.org/publications/fund-reports/2014/jun/mirror-mirror-wall-2014-update-how-us-health-care-system.
8. Health information technology for economic and clinical health act (HITECH Act): Wikipedia. Retrieved from https://en.wikipedia.org/wiki/Health_Information_Technology_for_Economic_and_Clinical_Health_Act.
9. Reisman, M. (2017, September). EHR's: The challenge of making electronic data usable and interoperable. *Pharmacy and Therapeutics*, 42(9), 572–575.
10. Kroth, P.J., Morioka-Douglas, N.M., Veres, S., et al. (2019). Association of electronic health record design and use factors with clinician stress and burnout. *JAMA Network Open*, 2(8), e199609. doi:10.1001/jamanetworkopen.2019.9609.
11. Gawande, A. (2018, November 12). *Why Doctors Hate Their Computers.* Retrieved from https://www.newyorker.com/magazine/2018/11/12/why-doctors-hate-their-computers.

12. Kizzier-Carnahan, V. Frequency of passive EHR alerts in the ICU, work on health and science university. Retrieved from https://ohsu.pure.elsevier.com/en/publications/frequency-of-passive-ehr-alerts-in-the-icu-another-form-of-alert-.
13. Caliri, A. (2019, January). The case for virtual scribes. *Beckers Hospital Review*. Retrieved from https://www.beckershospitalreview.com/hospital-physician-relationships/the-case-for-virtual-scribes.html.
14. Schulte, F., & Fry, E. (2019, March 18). By 1000 clicks: Where electronic health records went wrong. *Fortune*. Retrieved from https://khn.org/news/death-by-a-thousand-clicks/.
15. ICD 10 Wikipedia. Retrieved from https://en.wikipedia.org/wiki/ICD-10.
16. Brown, N. (2015, October). Top 10 most hilarious codes in ICD 10. Retrieved from https://www.nextech.com/blog/top-10-most-hilarious-codes-in-icd-10.
17. 2020 ICD– 10– CM diagnoses code 150.9. Retrieved from https://www.icd10data.com/ICD10CM/Codes/I00-I99/I30-I52/I50-/I50.9.
18. Calendar year(CY) 2019 medicare physician fee schedule (PSF) final rule. Retrieved from https://www.cms.gov/About-CMS/Story-Page/CY-19-PFS-Final-Rule-PPT.pdf.
19. Spitzer, J. (2018, July 11). *6 Stats on EHR-Related Physician Burnout and 7 Tips to Combat It*. Retrieved from https://www.beckershospitalreview.com/ehrs/6-stats-on-ehr-related-physician-burnout-and-7-tips-to-combat-it.html.
20. Cohen, J.K. (2018, November). Physician viewpoint: How to remove stupid stuff from the EHR, ACS communications 2018. Retrieved from https://www.beckershospitalreview.com/ehrs/physician-viewpoint-how-to-remove-stupid-stuff-from-ehrs.html.
21. Murphy, B. (2017, February). A burnout epidemic: 25 notes on physician burnout in the US, ACS Communications 2019. Retrieved from https://www.beckershospitalreview.com/hospital-management-administration/a-burnout-epidemic-25-notes-on-physician-burnout-in-the-us.html.
22. Kumar, R. (2018, September 6). *5 Ways to Reduce Physician Burnout Caused by EHRs*. Retrieved from https://www.softwareadvice.com/resources/reduce-physician-burnout/.
23. Devitt, M. (2019, January 16). *Study: EHRs Contribute to Family Physician Stress, Burnout*. Retrieved from https://www.aafp.org/news/practice-professional-issues/20190116ehrstudy.html.

24. *Electronic Health Records & Physician Burnout: Reversing a Dangerous Trend.* (2017, November 14). Retrieved from http://www.metacaresolutions.com/2017/11/electronic-health-records-physician-burnout-reversing-dangerous-trend/.
25. Hasan, H., & Kuzmanovich, D. (2018, May 16). *The Solution to Physician Burnout? EHR Optimization.* Retrieved from https://www.advisory.com/research/medical-group-strategy-council/practice-notes/2018/05/physician-burnout.
26. Henry, T.A. (2019, February 22). *Everybody Has Responsibilities for Fixing EHRs.* Retrieved from https://www.ama-assn.org/practice-management/digital/everybody-has-responsibilities-fixing-ehrs.
27. Landi, H. (2019, April 16). *First-Year Doctors Spend 3 Times More Hours on EHRs Than Patient Care.* Retrieved from https://www.fiercehealthcare.com/tech/first-year-doctors-spend-three-times-more-hours-ehrs-than-patient-care.
28. *Mayo Study Links EHRs with Physician Burnout.* (2016, June 28). Retrieved from https://www.beckershospitalreview.com/healthcare-information-technology/mayo-study-links-ehrs-with-physician-burnout.html.
29. Monica, K. *EHR Usability, Workflow Strategies for Reducing Physician Burnout.* Retrieved from https://ehrintelligence.com/features/ehr-usability-workflow-strategies-for-reducing-physician-burnout.
30. Runge, M.S. (2018, January 5). *Opinion: It's Time to Treat Physician Burnout's Root Causes.* Retrieved from https://labblog.uofmhealth.org/industry-dx/opinion-its-time-to-treat-physician-burnouts-root-causes.
31. Siwicki, B. (2019, January 29). *Can EHRs' Contributions to Physician Burnout Be Cured? Mixing Up Training Can Help.* Retrieved from https://www.healthcareitnews.com/news/can-ehrs'-contributions-physician-burnout-be-cured-mixing-training-can-help.
32. Strongwater, S. (2017, July 12). *Physicians Are Facing an EMR Burnout Crisis.* Retrieved from https://catalyst.nejm.org/videos/physicians-facing-crisis-emr-burnout/.
33. Wachter, R., & Goldsmith, J. (2018, March 30). *To Combat Physician Burnout and Improve Care, Fix the Electronic Health Record.* Retrieved from https://hbr.org/2018/03/to-combat-physician-burnout-and-improve-care-fix-the-electronic-health-record.

Chapter 9

Creating Resiliency and Grit

Bruce Flareau

Contents

Creating resiliency and grit in an organization requires the support of executive leadership, resources to be successful and a genuine desire on behalf of the system to shift the culture. The work involves helping individuals in their personal development efforts and retooling the work environment to make it easier for individuals to practice medicine, to be meaningfully engaged and to become fulfilled in their work. Dr. Tait Shanafelt has made an outstanding contribution to this work with his revelation that burnout is fundamentally NOT an individual problem triggered by personal limitations but instead is a system-level problem ground in the demands of overwork and inadequate resources and support.[1, 2] Others such as

Dr. Zubin Damania (ZDoggMD) argue it is a moral injury that results from clinicians having to commit or witness acts that violate their moral belief system. This linkage between what the environment produces and the individual's reaction to it results in the burnout we see. In addition, there is an increasing level of data showing that individual resiliency makes a difference and enables people to adapt better and tolerate challenges while working through solutions. Each is linked by a need to have a sense of purpose in one's life inclusive of their work and each has implicit relevance in determining where health systems should invest to help providers emerge from this national epidemic.

System-Level Initiatives

As discussed earlier in this book, systems are increasingly feeling the pressure to be more efficient, to deliver greater value to their patients and communities, and to continually grow, survive and to fulfill their organizational missions. Mergers and acquisitions are commonplace in the healthcare industry and with each stage of growth comes a greater burden on how best to meaningfully engage physicians at the local level. Whether it involves regional mergers or multistate systems, the challenges are real and complex. By the very nature of increasing scale, decisions are made by less and less people relative to the total workforce of physicians in any given system. Hence, creating an environment where every voice matters, and every physician feels a part of the solution is complex and daunting. Yet there are key things systems and physicians can do to not only mitigate but thrive in order to improve resiliency and grit.

First and foremost is making it easier for physicians to practice their chosen medical specialty. This may involve implementing scribes, using advanced care practitioners, streamlining workflows, and certainly looking at how to make the electronic medical record more user friendly. In almost every survey that has been published, the burden of the electronic medical record stands front and center as a challenge that imparts workflow dissatisfaction. Involving the physicians in the work redesign and eliminating non-value-added steps in the informatics arena are labor-intensive efforts but necessary to reduce the burdens upon the physicians. Systems can and should raise expectations from technology vendors such that new and existing technologies take physician workflows into account. During electronic medical record installations, it was not uncommon to hear physician complaints regarding click rates and redundant workflow actions. The cumulative effect of these challenges has taken its toll and it is a good place for any system to begin their work.

Second is the need to create organizational cultures that expect and even demand that physicians are engaged in establishing their own clinical standards, as well as their performance and practice expectations. All of this is in service to helping the physicians regain an increased sense of meaning and purpose in their work. This cultural work is paramount to long-term sustainability and those systems that make this transition will sustainably reap the rewards for years to come.

Physician Disillusionment and Physician Engagement

Physicians are typically viewed as individuals with a calling to help people. Historically, they have also been selected into medical school and residencies based upon their independent thinking, raw intelligence, and ego strength to withstand the rigors of training. The training process reinforced these attributes, thus creating confident strong-willed autocratic-type providers. While this has changed in recent years, there is still a great deal of independence and autocratic thinking in the current provider workforce as it was once a necessary attribute to assure success. Today, however, we are asking these highly trained strong-willed individuals to function in teams and to be good teammates. This cultural shift is happening across our industry and is not new information. Medical schools have been looking at elements of emotional intelligence and not just IQ as entrance criteria. Schools have group-based learning communities to foster a sense of team. Yet the ultimate decisions, good or bad and in cooperation with the patient, rests with the physician. As such, many physicians feel the burden of this responsibility and for them it weighs heavy. Changing long engrained attributes of individuality, coupled with this sense of ultimate responsibility, make this transformation more difficult for physicians.

Yet this rapidly changing industry fueled by consumerism, rising demands for quality and safety, and the cost of healthcare for payers, employers, and individuals is driving this need for change. These external influences are beyond the reach of a single physician and for some this leads to disillusionment. They may pine for the "good old days" or perhaps resist these forces and withdraw further and further from mainstream medicine. In 2019, the physician workforce crossed the 50% mark in which more physicians are now employees than are those practicing as independent providers. The dye has been set and resist as some might, change continues to happen. We are not advocating to try to resist change but rather that we raise awareness regarding the mindset of the physician as some feel they are increasingly losing control over the very practice of medicine. Team-based care is foreign, protocolized medicine is seen as a "cook book," and individualized patient-by-patient care feels compromised.

Helping these providers move forward means helping them see the virtues of this new care delivery system, engaging them in the very design of the future and certainly in acknowledging the essence of the change that is happening around and to them. Helping them understand "the why" can for some create insights and show them the path forward.

To help the reader gain a better sense of understanding as to why clinical standardization and care pathways may contribute to a sense of personal disillusionment, let us expand upon the physician mindset. Let us also suggest steps to enroll the physicians in both assisting with the change and simultaneously improving their own resiliency.

First, we need to come to grips with the reality that most of what is done in healthcare is not evidence based. More specifically, it is rare that we use strong science to definitively guide the care decisions made by the physician. In the realm of clinical research, this would be dubbed the double-blinded, placebo-controlled randomized study and/or the strongly weighted meta-analysis that give us a definitive answer as to how to provide care. Some readers may find this shocking, that much of the care delivered is still unclear with no perfect answer for every situation. Clearly, the body of evidence continues to grow, and answers are coming but physicians are largely aware that more than 80% of care delivered involves consensus-based care, snippets of extrapolated data, and many thousands of studies each contradicting the other.

And so, asking physicians to consistently practice to a standard is sometimes seen as insulting, demeaning, or even ridiculous to some when the provider takes the position that so much of what they do is without a single acceptable answer and therefore difficult to protocolize. When systems fail to recognize this aspect of care, and demand clinical standards in the absence of extensive practicing physician engagement, they may unwittingly contribute to self-fulfilling cycles of disillusionment for the physician. The more the physician intellectually pushes back on the standards, the more of an outlier they appear to be and the more isolated they sometimes become. Seeing this for what it is can give a glimpse into the necessary steps needed to systematically combat the issue.

There is, however, good news on the care standards front. One very successful health system messaged and, working with their practicing physicians, set the expectations that physicians are not only expected to practice to a clinical standard that they developed, but that they are equally expected to vary from those standards denoting and documenting situationally specific patient care attributes that call for the necessary variation. This dual messaging, which may seem subtle to some, is felt to be essential in creating buy-in as a change management vehicle, and in reaffirming the critical thinking skills of physicians and therefore instilling a sense of meaning and purpose in their professional roles.

Second, and overlapping with this idea of engaging practicing physicians to create local accountability, is the need to have them equally engaged in the creation of the accountability performance metrics as well. Classic teachings from Edward Deming, Joseph Juran, and other godfathers of quality improvement teach us that to improve we need to measure. Hence, many efforts are made to measure physician performance including productivity, effectiveness, and quality. As a result, thousands of dashboards of clinical performance have been produced, many based upon imperfect expectations of clinical evidence as this is the state of this industry. Engaging physicians to develop metrics that make sense to them and to which they will hold one another accountable creates buy-in, increases engagement, and aids in compliance and resiliency. And so here too we see a triple payoff in engaging our physicians in determining their fate; we believe the system wins, the patient wins and the individual physician wins.

To begin this transition toward meaningful engagement, it is helpful to begin to develop and showcase the many virtues of this evolving new delivery model including team-based care and performance accountability – each in service to helping the physician regain a sense of control in their lives and underscore purpose and meaning in their work. This messaging again is intended to sensitize the reader to the needs of the physician. Some examples of exceptional team-based care would include the ability to defray the long work hours that once prevailed as certain tasks can be done by others, while preserving or perhaps even improving the patient care experience or outcomes. Rather than expending energies marginalizing other members of the team, the resilient physician begins to see the team as advocates to improve their own workday and care delivery capabilities. Other examples could include messaging how adherence to clinical standards is a protection from malpractice – even if the patient experienced an adverse event!

And so, for systems to have an awareness of these challenges and to take a systems approach to improving them, will go a long way in removing the blame game and in beginning to create a culture of sustainable care delivery that addresses the workplace challenges that face our physicians. A recipe for success begins with creating an awareness that it is hard and complex to practice medicine while satisfying all the various agencies that exist. With this awareness in hand, the next phase of development is to invite the physicians into the conversation to create an environment in which their opinions matter and they know it and they feel it. Don't underestimate the last part of that statement. Yes, they have to feel that their voices matter. This emotional connection is critical. Some systems may have the intent to include physicians in decisions that affect their ability to practice medicine, but the felt impact may be anything but. Does your organization know how your providers feel about their voice in the process? If not, we would suggest it is worth examining. We contend that truly engaging physicians and making their voices heard will reap benefits for the system, for the patients, and for the physicians' own sense of purpose and well-being.

One highly regarded health system had its board pass a resolution that essentially said they would not make decisions that impact physician workflow without first involving practicing physicians in the process. This was like the shot heard round the world. It did not get the traction it needed until it was tested and validated. A technology solution, specifically an endoscopy documentation system, was selected with little-to-no physician input. Once identified, the initiative was stopped, the physicians engaged, and a different and more expensive solution prevailed with the commitment of the physicians that the solution would enable them to deliver better care. The physicians were willing to track that care and act upon outliers to deliver better outcomes. With this commitment, the system moved forward with the physician's recommendation. The physicians were shocked and amazed that the health system listened to them. The care improved, and their sense of purpose sky rocketed as measured through a standardized instrument. They saw and felt the change and it made all the difference in that culture. This set the tone for the organization and shifted the culture in a more aligned and fruitful way. Case studies such as this show that this approach of engagement is effective at combating disillusionment.

External Validation

Note that our recommendations thus far relate to eliminating barriers and creating a greater sense of meaning and purpose. They have not spoken to things such as compensation, titles, or other external benefits of reward or validation. Current thinking looks at resiliency in terms of things that enhance and those things that detract from the creation and sustenance of resiliency.[3, 5] As it relates to external factors, we also know that eliminating barriers to practice great medicine outweighs efforts related to title and money. This has been well articulated by Drs Tom Lee and Deirdre Mylod in their February 4, 2019, *JAMA* article, "Deconstructing burnout to define a positive path forward." They discuss rewards and stresses inherent to the role of caring for patients. They further define inherent factors versus those that are added from their work or other environments. They use this model to underscore the importance of making it easier to practice medicine in the course of a day or week.

	Rewards	*Stress/Distress*
Environmental (System/ Organization)	• Income • Benefits • Prestige • Recognition • Inclusivity • Belonging	• Burdensome processes • On call • Productivity • EMR • Schedules • Information overload
Inherent (Individual/ Core)	• Meaning/purpose • Feeling of inclusivity • Affirmation/ appreciation • Social context • Reconnecting with our core	• Ultimate responsibility • Isolation • Witness to suffering • Desire for excellence • Complexity

* Adapted from ***JAMA*** 2019 Feb. "Deconstructing Burnout to Define a Positive Path Forward," Tom Lee, MD, Deirdre Mylod, PhD, Copyright Press Ganey.

Many physicians have described their work environments like those of a hamster running inside of a hamster wheel. Never making headway yet the speed of the wheel continually going faster and faster.

Interestingly enough, primary care physicians who exist in the fee-for-service environments are particularly prone to this feeling of speed and loss of control. Systems have contributed to this by requiring metrics of productivity, RVU compensation models, limiting overhead resources and pressuring physicians with governmental and other measures of quality often seen as arbitrary by the very physicians and patients they impact. Conversely, physicians who have made the transition to full capitation or concierge practices have at times regained a sense of control by limited panel sizes and slower paced days. Systems need to assist physicians with this transformation rather than having physicians try to co-exist in both financial models. Thus "one foot in each canoe" model is contributing to the challenges and pushing through the transformation will aid in developing resiliency.

In addition to these operational flow and cultural areas, systems can aid in the creation of physician communities. Some systems have allocated dinner funding to allow physicians to reconnect after hours of work and establish social groups. This "tribe-like" behavior has assisted in information sharing, social support structures, a greater sense of belonging, and an overall enhanced sense of general well-being. And finally, systems need to establish cultures where all operational decisions are examined to determine the impact upon physician workflows prior to implementation.

Individual-Focused Programs

As discussed above, investing in the core attributes of our clinical workforce has been shown to improve resiliency and patient care quality and safety. These programs vary in depth and facilitator experience. The ideal program is led by an experienced facilitator either in a group or in one-on-one settings and helps clinicians examine their lives in total and to develop a life plan that assists them in reconnecting with their core, investing in their own joy and happiness and finding solutions for themselves. This work often begins with attention to the physicians' own health and wellness. Neglecting their health can create a downward spiral and is often seen with poor diet, limited to no exercise routines, and variation from the very self-care recommendations they expect of their patients. Personal life development programs often involve the use of an executive coach. With a horizontally motivated workforce, the willingness of an employer to invest in its individuals in this capacity may create loyalties yet to be fully determined. Certainly, turnover is costly and efforts to lower it, such as coaching and personal development planning, have shown to have a return on investments. And so group coaching, individual coaching, personal development plans, and supportive cultures to allow this work to occur are powerful ingredients in making the necessary shifts for any system wanting to improve resiliency, eliminate burnout, and create vital work environments that lower errors and deliver better care for patients.

Additional justification for work in this realm rests upon a foundational belief that creating the capacity to take on challenges of any kind is dependent upon having a solid foundation in one's own life. Hence in this way of thinking, resiliency is not limited to the work environment but instead is the accumulation of capacity across all aspects of one's life. The more connected someone is with their sense of "core," we believe the better positioned they are to adapt and overcome challenges. While there are many models looking at the landscape of one's life, all have several aspects in common. Attending to one's professional development and financial well-being are just one sphere of influence. Family, significant other, spirituality, fun, recreation, and personal health and wellness are others. As one reconnects with their core and builds a foundation of strength across these various life components, they are better equipped to absorb challenges as they occur.

In summary, creating resiliency and grit is not a single linear process. Instead, it involves removing obstacles to providing excellent care, creating cultures of appreciation and reestablishing a sense of pride and purpose in the workplace all while helping individuals reconnect with their core and establish life plans that work for them. This work begins in medical school and should carry through graduate education and into practice. EHR vendors and regulators alike should collaborate with physicians to make a useable system with greater interoperability. Health systems should invest in leadership to drive these programs and to shape their cultures. A systems approach needs to be adopted, inclusive of practicing physicians and solutions that improve workflows and enhance care delivery. Together, these types of initiatives will drive the culture and the workplace toward healthier, happier, more resilient physicians and providers and therefore translate to safer and better-quality care.

Bibliography

1. West, C.P, Dyrbye, L.N., Erwin, P.J., & Shanafelt, T.D. (2016, September 28). Interventions to prevent and reduce physician burnout: A systematic review and meta-analysis. *Lancet, 388.*
2. Tait, Shanafelt, Goh, Joel, & Sinsky, Christine. (2017, September 25). The business case for investing in physician well-being. *JAMA.*
3. Thomas, Lee, & Mylod, Deirdre. (2019, February 4). Deconstructing burnout to define a positive path forward. *JAMA, 179*(3), 429–430.
4. Jha, Ashish, Iliff, A.R., & Chaoui, A.A. A crisis in health care: A call to action on physician burnout. *White Paper.*
5. MylodDeirdre. (2017, October 12). One way to prevent physician burnout. *Harvard Business Review.* Retrieved from https://hbr.org/2017/10/one-way-to-prevent-physician-burnout.
6. Dyrbye, L.N., Shanafelt, T.D., & Sinsky, C.A., et al. (2017, July 5). Burnout among healthcare providers: A call to explore and address this underrecognized threat to safe, high-quality care. *National Academy of Medicine.* Discussion Paper, pp. 1–11.

Chapter 10

Burnout in Nurses across Practice Domains: Implications and Correlations to Physician Burnout

Kathleen Ferket

Contents

We are planning to identify factors which contribute to nursing burnout and if or how they correspond to physician burnout. As discussed in previous chapters, physician burnout is a growing epidemic influenced by many diverse factors. However, nursing burnout impacts healthcare in equally a serious manner. Just like physicians, individuals pursuing a nursing degree are highly intelligent, intrinsically motivated and generally considered hardy and resilient enough to withstand the high expectations of training and preparation. We will compare burnout implications across various nursing roles, including acute care nurses at the bedside, advanced practice providers (APPs), and the Chief Nursing Executive. Common denominators which contribute to both nursing and physician burnout in today's practice environment will be discussed.

The Bedside Nurse

Bedside nurses in acute care hospitals are on the front line of healthcare. Although practice settings vary, such as the emergency department, medical surgical unit, behavioral health, intensive care unit or procedural areas, each setting brings its own set of distinct clinical challenges. Patients in hospitals are more acutely ill than in years past. Clinical staff and administrators are intensely focused on managing clinical outcomes which include patient safety, quality, patient experience, patient length of stay, and nursing productivity. Factor in ever-changing technology, equipment alarms, and empowered consumers with specific treatment expectations, the combined ingredients contribute to a highly stressful environment. Managing the daily stress and expectations of this high-tech, high-touch environment is integral to maintaining individual resilience and a hardiness factor to survive in healthcare today.

Education and Onboarding

Nursing is a highly desired career and attracts individuals who are intelligent, caring, motivated, and drawn to "make a difference." The *promise* of making a positive difference for patients is a common and profound mission for new nurses. The demand for nurses is high but nursing school enrollment is at capacity and promising students are turned away, due to faculty shortages. Nursing faculty shortages have existed for decades, related to lower academic salary structures. The nursing curriculum is complex, consisting of both didactic and clinical rotations which are required to meet rigorous accreditation standards. Nursing shortages exist worldwide while job stress, dissatisfaction, lack of peer support, and limited professional opportunities still contribute to attrition.[10]

Unlike medical students and residents, the student nurse exposure in clinical rotations is "protected" with an instructor nearby, a lower patient assignment, and the understanding that unit staff nurse maintains the overall accountability for the patient. Difficult encounters with patients, families, physicians, or other clinicians are much less likely to occur without the nursing instructor or staff nurse assigned to the patient taking the lead. Fostering "protection" in nursing clinical rotations is common but ultimately not helpful for the new nurse. As the first difficult and crucial conversation encounter occurs, which may be accusatory, bullying, belittling, or all the above, the nurse may retreat, cry, and internalize feelings of failure. Introducing the communication skills to deal effectively with clear but *difficult* conversations in a simulated environment will prove very useful to new nurses.

Many organizations offer a nurse residency program and trained preceptor programming to create a positive clinical learning environment and entry into practice. Unfortunately, not all organizations support this evidence-based approach, primarily due to cost restraints. Nurse residency programs have been around since the 1980s but adoption and continued commitment require both administrative and financial support.[1] The experience of precepting a new graduate is a huge responsibility and usually is uncompensated. As simulation training expands and clinical rotations are limited, a newly graduated nurse is expected to gain additional, "on-the-job" experience in the acute care setting, alongside a preceptor to guide her in the early stages of her career. Ensuring a well-qualified preceptor is important to the retention of newly graduated nurses.

Staffing

Nurse staffing in acute care has moved primarily to a 12-hour shift model. This has contributed to nurse satisfaction, especially for full-time employees who desire additional time off. However, a 12-hour shift schedule has additional implications, especially when it comes to continuity of care and patient safety. Consecutive 12-hour shifts (36–40 hours) provide the nurse with additional time off but can leave the nurse physically and mentally exhausted. The 12-hour shift offers the flexibility for a nurse to work additional shifts at a second job, compounding fatigue and stress. If shift rotation is factored in, it adds additional stress on nurses, all of which contribute to burnout.

Policies related to the number of worked hours in a specific timeframe are in place in organizations. However, compliance and monitoring of the policy may be variable and oversight may be at the department level and applied inconsistently. High census, high acuity, or staffing shortages may present a situation when staffing requirements may be modified, or simply disregarded. If a nurse declines to work extra, it can contribute to anguish, especially if it involves a concern regarding patient safety or, if they are made to feel guilty about not picking up a shift by a coworker or supervisor.

The longer the shift, the greater the likelihood of adverse nurse outcomes, which further contribute to burnout. Patients were less satisfied with their care when there were higher proportions of nurses working shifts of 13 or more hours but were more satisfied when there were higher proportions of nurses working 11 or fewer hours.[12]

Culture and Environment

A positive organizational culture influences successful onboarding and contributes to both nurse retention and reduced turnover. Magnet hospitals offer a framework for structural empowerment, shared governance and demonstrate positive outcomes to retain nurses. Many new nurses will apply to hospitals that attain Magnet status. However, the Magnet program is a substantial financial investment for both new and renewing organizations. Magnet designation is positively correlated to improved patient outcomes, nurse satisfaction, and staffing. Despite strong research supporting both Magnet and nurse residency programs, these programs are expensive and becoming difficult to sustain in the current financially orientated healthcare environment.

Lateral Violence (Bullying)

The phrase, "nurses eat their young" has been around for a very long time. Experienced nurses can be especially tough on new graduates, as well as medical students and residents. Despite research done regarding *Lateral Violence* and *Just Culture*, bullying practices continue to exist in organizations. In some cases, nurse bullying is the result of ineffective communication and coping skills in a high stakes environment. Lateral violence is also seen with physicians, police officers, and teachers. There are still some mentors who believe that if they are hard on new nurses, it will help them become more competent and stronger overall care providers. The problem with that training tactic is that it sidesteps the theory that competence comes from *confidence*.[9] A zero tolerance policy for lateral violence in any manner as well as education regarding professional and respectful communication must be implemented across the organization. As in real-life situations, fear of retaliation for reporting such behavior may dissuade nurses from pursuing organizational options. This can contribute to propagating the cycle of violence.

Organizational Cost of Nursing

Nursing is the largest workforce in the acute care setting and has 24/7 accountability for patient safety, medication delivery, recognizing and responding to patient status changes, supporting families in crisis and yet, as professionals, their contributions do not generate *direct* revenue for a hospital. This situation is the primary reason nurse staffing is usually a precarious target during budget planning and reduction in force initiatives. Aside from case managers, in general, most nurses have a limited understanding of how a hospital gets paid. While physicians receive education on payment/reimbursement, coding, and billing on their practices, they too have a lack of understanding regarding hospital payments.

As a profession, nursing has struggled over the years to quantify its value, especially as it relates to the revenue cycle of financial management. In 2019, nursing costs are still rolled into a room and board item charged on a patient bill. This, along with many other factors, has contributed to a lack of autonomy, fosters disempowerment, and in some cases, a lack of respect from other disciplines. Lack of autonomy and disempowerment are strong contributors to burnout.[11] Merriam Webster defines disillusion as *the condition of being disenchanted: the condition of being dissatisfied or defeated in expectation or hope.*[7] Edelwich and Brodsky described burnout in the helping professions as a process of increasing disillusionment, the "progressive loss of idealism, energy, and purpose experienced by people in the helping professions as a result of conditions of their work."[9]

Currently, nurse educators must incorporate a fundamental understanding of the hospital revenue cycle in the curriculum. There is no profession that is as unprepared as nursing is to understand how their product/skill generates revenue for their services.

Summary

New nurses may experience culture shock as they transition into practice, largely because they are insufficiently prepared for the reality, pace, expectations, and demands of practicing at the bedside. Do nursing programs contribute to nurse burnout by glossing over challenges new nurses may encounter when they enter clinical practice? There is an immediate opportunity to discuss *practical expectations* regarding the true work of nurses in a hospital environment.

Tenured nurses at the bedside either leave or adapt to the acute care setting. Components of resilience for nurses at the bedside include maintaining strong connections with family and friends, nurture a positive view of yourself, practice self-care activities, take actions to move toward goals, avoid seeing crises as insurmountable problems and accept that change.[4]

In 2018, the turnover rate for bedside RNs grew to 17.2% and tied CY2015 as the highest in the past decade. According to the survey, the average cost of turnover for a bedside RN is $52,100 and ranges from $40,300 to $64,000 resulting in the average hospital losing $4.4 to $6.9 million. Each percent change in RN turnover will cost/save the average hospital an additional $328,400. Over 20% (22.9%) of all new RNs left within a year. First year turnover accounted for over a quarter (27.7%) of all RN separations.[8]

Currently, healthcare is experiencing profound change. Focusing on strategies to enhance resilience and improve effective communication in all bedside nurses is very important and may prevent turnover, or worse yet, prevent a talented clinician from leaving the profession.

A proactive investment in onboarding and a commitment to supporting continued growth and resilience in both new and experienced nurses will go a long way to positively impact clinician well-being, patient quality and care (Table 10.1).

Table 10.1 Describes potential drivers for nurse burnout, identifies correlations to physician burnout, and lists considerations to minimize burnout

Contributing Factors	*Physician Interrelated*	*Suggestions/Discussion*
Inadequate staffing	Yes	Nurse staffing committees, leader support to attend
Inadequate or interrupted breaks	Yes	Team/leader support for breaks; outside garden access for breaks/lunch
Lateral violence/bullying	Yes	Just Culture Framework, interprofessional relationships, communication, zero tolerance policy adherence, cultural competency, resiliency screening

(Continued)

Table 10.1 (Continued) Describes potential drivers for nurse burnout, identifies correlations to physician burnout, and lists considerations to minimize burnout

Contributing Factors	*Physician Interrelated*	*Suggestions/Discussion*
Moral distress, compassion fatigue	Yes	Schwartz Rounds, debriefing session after significant event, recognition of second victim events, resiliency screening
PTSD	Yes	Debriefing post significant events, support group, meditation, exercise, resiliency screening
EMR related	Yes	Representation on Informatics committee, adequate computer stations, biometric single sign on, IT supportive of suggestions
Inadequate orientation	Variable	Formal preceptor programs, nurse residency programs
Toxic environment	Yes	Nursing wellness committee
Shift rotation, excessive overtime	Yes	Workforce policies regarding consecutive shifts, safety education

Advanced Practice Providers

Introduction

Two professional roles are included in the Advanced Practice Provider category: Advanced Practice Registered Nurse (APRN) and Physician Assistant (PA). The primary focus of this discussion will be directed toward the APRN, but similar underlying factors contributing to burnout are true for the Physician Assistant, as well.

APRNs include nurse practitioners, clinical nurse specialists, nurse anesthetists, and nurse midwives, and all play a pivotal role in the future of health care. APRNs are often primary care providers and are at the forefront of providing preventive care services to the public.[8] APRNs may diagnose illness, develop and manage treatment plans, prescribe medications, and may serve as a patient's principal healthcare provider. Preparation includes a master's degree and specific specialty clinical hours. The pathway to independent practice for APPs is happening across the United States.

PAs are medical professionals who diagnose illness, develop and manage treatment plans, prescribe medications, and often serve as a patient's principal healthcare provider. Preparation includes a 2-year plus program, approximately 2,000 clinical hours, and matriculate with a master's degree. The scope of practice is evolving for PAs but requirements for collaborative practice with physicians vary from state to state.

All APPs must obtain certification, maintain a separate license, and complete all required continuing education credits, based on their state rules and regulations. Both APRN and PA programs began in the mid-sixties in response to a shortage of physicians, especially in underserved populations and regions.

Implications Contributing to APP Burnout

Medical staff acceptance of APPs has been a long and difficult road, and in some cases the journey to the top of APP license continues to be a challenge. The organizations and physicians who were "early adopters" of the APP role recognized their importance in supporting and providing patient care and helped champion their use. The sad reality is, there are still physicians who do not see the value, and their confirmation bias may never be resolved. Many physicians feel threatened by APPs which is unfortunate, because they offer the opportunity to collaborate in a team-based model of care.

Despite the longevity of the APP role, a lack of understanding regarding APP practice capability remains. In particular, the APRN role grew *organically*, especially in acute care settings, as organizations designed roles to meet specific gaps in care. This contributed to APRNs practice variation and not practicing to their full scope of practice potential.

Role ambiguity is a long-standing problem for APPs which does not exist for physicians. Justification regarding the APP role and expertise continues, despite research and data supporting the positive impact of APPs on clinical outcomes, such as patient satisfaction, safety, cost effectiveness and access to care. Both APRNs and PAs agree on the classification of advanced practice provider, but terms such as "mid-level provider" and "physician extender" continue to be used, even though they are outdated and diminish the expertise of today's well-educated and trained advanced practice provider.

Practicing at top of license is an ongoing opportunity for all APPs. Healthcare entities are working to justify both the cost and use of APPs. Medical staff executive committees have expanded to include APP representatives, usually as a nonvoting member. Credentialing of the APP to the hospital medical staff continues to advance slowly. In many locations, including an APP representative in the credentialing process has improved the process for peer review and endorsement.

Employment

Further contributing to the confusion regarding APPs is employment status. APPs may be directly employed by a physician practice or may be employed through the hospital entity. Often, there is no way to differentiate this employment status which can be confusing to other clinicians in the practice setting. APPs will need to consistently communicate their scope of practice, while at the same time, avoiding any *defensive posturing* regarding the need to reinforce the message. Contract negotiation is an important component to ensure adequate compensation. For new APPs entering practice, a contract that does not provide adequate benefits or paid time off may contribute to dissatisfaction and additional stress or burnout.

The Chief Nursing Executive has accountability and oversight for nursing in their organization and often this will include APRNs. There is often a dual reporting structure with the CMO or other physicians. It is vital that APRNs ensure the CNE is current on all license and scope of practice considerations. It is a best practice for the CNE to be involved in the APP hospital credentialing, as well as the Chief Medical Officer. The CNE should be knowledgeable regarding APRN top of license capability so they can be an advocate for the most effective use of the professional.

APP Onboarding

There is a trend of bedside nurses moving into advance practice roles, related to the demands associated with acute care workload, as well as the opportunity for improved autonomy. The transition from staff nurse to APRN is stressful related to increased expectations and accountability. Providing mentorship and a structured onboarding program is key to satisfaction and retention of APPs. Many organizations are instituting APP governance structures which include credentialing, interviewing, and onboarding. If the APP is contracted by a physician practice, the onboarding may be tailored to the individual physician or practice setting. As with the new staff nurse, a new APP will be more successful with a formalized orientation and a designated preceptor.

APP Summary

Interprofessional relationships and clear communication are essential to the success of APPs, despite their practice setting or employment. Development of an APP leadership structure, with representatives from both the APRN and PA sector, will help with burnout reduction. Some organizations have identified APRN and PA leaders to represent and provide input on key organizational committees. An APP wellness committee is a good starting point for identifying opportunities to mitigate stress and provide options for improving resilience. Routine resilience assessments should be a part of annual evaluations or performance assessments.

Continued education regarding the APP role is necessary for physicians, nurses, support teams as well as the consumer. An organizational annual APP report is a good method to highlight achievements, presentations, publications, and patient stories.

Table 10.2 demonstrates the potential drivers for APP burnout, identifies the factors which correlate to physician burnout, and lists potential considerations for managing burnout.

Table 10.2 APP burnout table

Contributing Factors	*Physician Interrelated*	*Suggestions/Discussion*
Highly motivated, caring individuals	Yes	APP participation on wellness council; bi-monthly reciliencey monitoring with validated assessment tool; move APP to performance-based compensation model
Role ambiguity	No	APP leadership council; APP annual report; communication regarding APP outcomes
Role expectations	Yes	APP structured onboarding programs; clear scope of practice
Workload, schedules, long shifts	Yes	APP workforce council; education regarding employment contracts
Patient expectations	Yes	APP patient brochure; seated at eye level of patient, family during discussions

(*Continued*)

Table 10.2 (Continued) APP burnout table

Contributing Factors	*Physician Interrelated*	*Suggestions/Discussion*
EMR Multiple sign on Multiple passwords Excessive documentation Application disconnect	Yes	APP representation on Informatics council Single biometric sign on Adequate computer access Voice recognition for dictation
High responsibility, low control	Yes	Ensure APP representatives on medical staff committees
Autonomy	+/−	Scope of practice outlined in employment contract or job description
Practice to top of license	No	APP organization structure, dyad reporting, continued monitoring of practice

Chief Nursing Executive Burnout

Introduction

Nurse leaders in executive practice set the strategy and vision for nursing practice in the delivery of safe, timely, efficient, equitable, and patient-centered care. Working within a collaborative and interprofessional environment, the nurse in executive practice is influential in improving the patient experience of care (including quality and satisfaction), improving the health of populations and reducing the per capita cost of health care.[3] The CNE requires a broad base of knowledge, including professionalism, leadership, business, strategy, marketing, technology, in addition to clinical knowledge and operations.

Burnout in the CNE is an ever-present risk and it is driven by a multitude of pressing demands and priorities. The CNE has accountability for the largest number of direct and indirect reports in the organization. A hospital cannot function without a 24-hour, 7 day a week complement of nursing staff and this responsibility is an ever-present stressor. The opportunity for organized labor to enter an organization, nursing turnover, staff reductions are continual challenges that contribute to CNE burnout.

Accountability for the clinical and regulatory accreditation cycle is a crucial area for the CNE. Mitigating organizational risk, adherence to federal and state requirements, ensuring professional staff licensure while achieving top accreditation and awards are a few of the very public responsibilities. Due to the broad span of control, the CNE holds accountability for achieving top clinical outcomes across the organization. To preserve the best staffing models, the savvy CNE requires excellent working relationships and the respect of the finance department.

Ensuring a healthy workplace environment and setting a tone for respectful communication and collaboration is an important role for the CNE. Despite daily challenges in healthcare, it is imperative civility and a zero tolerance for lateral violence are the expected norm throughout the organization. Along with the board of directors, c-suite, and physician leaders, the CNE works to align and enact the mission and values of the organization to the culture.

A respectful, collaborative, and dyad relationship between the CNE and the Chief Medical Officer is an important component to ensuring a healthy workplace for both physicians and all other clinicians. Healthcare entities have been and continue to be physician centric. The CNE and the nursing division must be held in the same standing as the CMO and the medical staff by the CEO and the hospital board. Creating this culture will be important to the CNE who strive to build a strong, collaborative nursing culture.

On average, about 100 hospital/system mergers or acquisitions occur every year.[13] The move toward population health and value-based care strategies are driving organizations to focus on cost, size, scale, and volume. The CNE must stay abreast of the rapidly changing healthcare landscape and support both leaders and staff during the anxious time of consolidation. The CNE will need to continually manage their own stress regarding an uncertain future, as reductions at the C suite level are often a part of a newly merged organization.

CNE Summary

The nurse leader has a vast scope of responsibility and accountability. Organizations are transitioning the CNE role, on average, about every three to five years and CNEs report the inability to effectively manage the growing number of competing priorities. At the same time, the pool of experienced CNEs is decreasing.[8] A new CNE may bring leadership changes, which in turn drive staff turnover and dissatisfaction, especially if staffing reductions are implemented. The stage for further burnout opportunity is set.

As the role model for professionalism and practice, it is imperative the CNE demonstrate the ability to foster a healthy work-life balance. Yet, how does the CNE manage the stress, expectations, and vast responsibilities of this role without potentially experiencing the phenomenon of burnout themselves? (Table 10.3)

Summary

Definitions of burnout indicate that burnout begins with stress, resulting from the discrepancy between the individual's expectations and ideals, and the harsh reality of everyday occupational life. It can include the development of negative attitudes

Table 10.3 Demonstrates the potential drivers for CNE burnout, identifies the interrelated aspects to physician burnout, and lists potential considerations for decreasing burnout

Contributing Factors	*Physician Interrelated*	*Suggestions/Discussion*
Highly motivated, caring individuals	Yes	Wellness council model
Span of control	No	Delegation and structural empowerment
High role expectations	Yes	Physical decompression, sleep, Appreciative Inquiry practice
Workload, 40–60+ weeks	Yes	Time management, vacations out of the country to ensure uninterrupted leisure time
Multiple stakeholders	Yes	Interprofessional collaboration and relationships
High responsibility, moderate control	Yes	Leadership, influence, respect of medical staff, and board
Autonomy	Yes	Empowered to decision-making, leadership attributes
Clinical outcomes	Yes	Participation in goal setting; data integrity
Moral distress	Yes	Schwartz Rounds, networking with peers, professional organizations

and frequently occurs among highly motivated individuals.[10] Individuals drawn to healthcare are mission driven and highly motivated.[11]

In the last 20 years, healthcare has transformed into a business, largely influenced by ever expanding technology and costs associated with education, practice, research, pharmaceuticals, and improvement in quality. This "business versus mission" disconnect is contributing to the disillusionment of clinicians across all settings.

But, healthcare as a business is not going away; it represents almost 20% of the Gross National Product for the United States. So, how do we bridge the discrepancy between healthcare as a business and healthcare as a calling?

Mounting scientific evidence shows that resilience is an *essential* component to overall health and well-being, and that with intentional cognitive or behavioral efforts, one can increase resilience levels[4]. Additional evidence demonstrates how resilience acts as a mediator for burnout in healthcare professionals.

The American Hospital Association has outlined a seven-step playbook for enhancing organizational well-being, which may help counteract clinician burnout.[2] In addition, areas to prevent burnout at all practice levels include adequate sleep, decompensation activities, and the development of moral resilience.

The ability to face pressures improves with increased sleep length and quality, resulting in higher performance. When leaders observe negative behaviors or reduced coping in colleagues, often inadequate sleep may be the issue.[5] Disconnecting from electronic devices and cell phones an hour or more before bedtime can help with ensuring proper sleep

The opportunity to decompress during physical activities is helpful in reducing stress. Unfortunately, for many professionals, decompressing with alcohol or opioids can contribute to additional problems that may compound burnout.

The practice of appreciative inquiry is helpful for clinicians and may enhance moral resilience. Appreciative inquiry is about the search for the best in people, their organizations, and the strengths-filled, opportunity-rich world around them.[6] Appreciative inquiry is not so much a shift in the methods and models of organizational change, but rather a fundamental shift in the overall perspective taken throughout the entire change process to "see" the wholeness of the human system and to "inquire" into that system's strengths, possibilities, and successes. While there will always be problems and demands, a paradigm shift of focusing first on what is going well, before tackling the questions/issues of what *is not* going well is a good first start.

Physicians, nurses, and administration set the cultural tone for the organization. This culture can affect everyone and if one group is struggling with high burnout, it can affect all others. Burnout is like a contagious disease, in that one group can influence and affect the entire organization. The strategies to prevent burnout must be adopted across the organization and each employee should be held accountable to the same standard. Since nursing is the largest employed group, it is critical nurses be evaluated for resiliency and symptoms of burnout but consideration should be given to managing and monitoring a resilience factor in all clinicians.

A Work-Life Balance assessment, along with a resilience assessment tool (Maslach), should be monitored and reviewed at least semiannually to identify opportunities for intervention. Organizations should move to reporting clinician well-being on their organizational dashboard. A well-being metric may be the impetus to further improve all other measures and has been incorporated in the Quadruple Aim.

For highly motivated physicians and nurses, working faster, harder, and longer is not a sustainable answer. Placing oneself first, instead of last, is a lesson we hear each time we travel by air. Put your own oxygen mask on first, before helping the child or individual next to you. As healthcare professionals, we must have the discipline to incorporate positive self-care activities into daily practice.

The American Hospital Association has identified key steps to foster organizational well-being.[2]

1. Create an infrastructure for well-being
2. Engage your team
3. Measure well-being

4. Design interventions
5. Implement programs
6. Evaluate program impact
7. Create a sustainable culture

The immediate call to action for healthcare executives, physicians, and nurses at every practice level is to hold one another accountable for instituting the steps to ensure a healthy workforce and culture. Each healthcare leader (physicians, nurses, APPs, CNEs, and administrators) must adopt practices that enhance their own resilience and role model these practices to their patients and families.

Bibliography

1. Anderson, G., Hair, C., & Todero, C. (2012, July–August). Nurse residency programs: An evidence-based review of theory, process, and outcomes. *Journal of Professional Nursing: Official Journal of the American Association of Colleges of Nursing, 28*(4), 203–212.
2. American hospital association, well being playbook. https://www.aha.org/system/files/media/file/2019/05/plf-well-being-playbook.pdf.
3. American organization of nurse leaders: Nurse executive competencies. (2015). https://www.aonl.org/system/files/media/file/2019/06/nec.pdf.
4. Bernard, N. (2019, February). Resilience and professional joy: A toolkit for nurse leaders. *Nurse Leader, 17*, 43–48.
5. https://www.apa.org/helpcenter/road-resilience#targetText=Pay%20attention%20to%20your%20own,with%20situations%20that%20require%20resilience.
6. https://appreciativeinquiry.champlain.edu/learn/appreciative-inquiry-introduction/.
7. https://www.merriam-webster.com/.
8. https://www.nursingworld.org/practice-policy/workforce/what-is-nursing/aprn/.
9. https://sigma.nursingrepository.org/handle/10755/603242.

10. 2019 national health care retention & RN staffing report, published by: NSI Nursing Solutions, Inc. www.nsinursingsolutions.com.
11. Schaufeli, W.B., & Buunk, B.P. (1996). Professional burnout, chapter 15. In: *Handbook of Work and Health Psychology*. John Wiley & Sons Ltd.
12. Stimpfel, A.W., Sloane, D.M., & Aiken, L.H. (2012, November). The longer the shifts for hospital nurses, the higher the levels of burnout and patient satisfaction. *Health Affairs*, *31*(11), 2501–2509.
13. https://www.fiercehealthcare.com/hospitals-health-systems/report-what-to-expect-healthcare-m-a-2019.

Chapter 11

Burnout: A Healthcare Crisis for Us All

George Mayzell and Bruce Flareau

Contents

The implications of burnout go far beyond the individual physician, healthcare organizations, and the individual patient. This problem is ubiquitous and affects directly or indirectly every physician, every healthcare worker, and everyone who needs healthcare either now or in the future. So essentially it affects everyone. It has been called a public health crisis.[1, 2]

As noted in earlier chapters, physicians are not the only ones experiencing burnout. Nurses' burnout experience ranges from 30% to 70%.[3]

In our opinion, the evidence is clear that burnout is an epidemic affecting the delivery of healthcare at every institution and every physician's office. Given the impact on the cost of healthcare, on patient safety, on the patient experience, and on access to healthcare, collectively we believe it has large societal impacts. It has been suggested that physician burnout costs the US healthcare industry between $2.6 billion and $6.3 billion a year, according to the study published by *Annals of Internal Medicine*. This is based on the cost of turnover, reduced productivity, and other burnout-related factors.[4]

According to Don Berwick, in the first era of medicine, "society ceded to the medical profession a privilege most workgroups do not get: the authority to judge the quality of its own work." The second and current era is dominated by rewards, punishments, and pay for performance." This results in a "collision of norms" between physicians' professional autonomy and the new era of accountability. This sums up many of the societal drivers of burnout.[1]

The First Step Is Raising Awareness

The first step in solving any problem is to acknowledge that there is a problem. While most individuals inside healthcare organizations are aware of this issue, it still has not reached a high level of public awareness. This is changing slowly. To date, it feels like the consequences of burnout have mostly been expressed in terms of what happens to the individual physician or the healthcare organization. Until the societal impacts become public knowledge, policy and compliance and other changes will be difficult to champion.

Collaboration – This Crisis Calls for Alignment of Medical Societies, the Government, the AMA, and Healthcare Leadership

An equally important step is having healthcare organizations; political organizations, such as the American Medical Association (AMA); state societies; and specialty societies all aligned and agreeing to solve the problem. They must all speak with the same voice so that the public hears a consistent and understandable message, including how it affects them directly. There is already an Action Collaborative Watch by the National Academy of Medicine consisting of 60 organizations.[5] In the viewpoint section of the March 7, 2019, issue of *JAMA, the Journal of the American Medical Association,* the Action Collaborative stated that "meaningful progress will require collaborative efforts by national bodies, healthcare organizations, leaders and individual physicians, as each is responsible for factors that contribute to the problem and must own their part of the solution. Solving this problem will require cooperation at every level of the healthcare system."[6] This needs to expand on a national and even international basis. This problem is not limited to the United States, although compliance and other regulatory restrictions accentuate it here.

One other important role that national organizations, such as the AMA, can and should take is to share best practices of burnout mitigation with the medical community. There is no reason that everyone should reinvent the wheel. There should be some economies of scale that sharing best practice and solutions across the nation should achieve. While they have put together some great resources that are valuable, there are still continued opportunities.[7]

National organizations can help us all agree on common metrics for burnout, engagement, and the other phenomena covered in this book. It is only through these commonly agreed-upon metrics that we can truly compare successes and failures and best assess what works and what does not.[8]

The Quadruple Aim

Several years ago, Don Berwick at the Institute of Healthcare Improvement (IHI) described the triple aim.[9] The triple aim suggests that healthcare should aspire to delivering care that improves patient experience, lowers unit cost, and improves the health of patients and populations; this is aspirational. More recently, the triple aim has been amended to include a fourth metric, physician and health worker burnout. This has now been called the quadruple aim. As we focus on this new agenda, it brings to light the criticality of looking at all of these four aspects of healthcare. Clearly, the emotionality and health of the delivery system is a critical factor necessary to deliver world-class healthcare (Figure 11.1).

Quadruple Aim

- Patient experience
- Reducing costs
- Health of a population
- Care team's well-being

Figure 11.1 The quadruple aim[9]

Cycle of Rising Costs

One of the largest challenges for society is the continued rise of healthcare costs in excess of the rise in gross domestic product. This continued rise is unsustainable. While there have been many attempts to try to control these costs, there are also many challenges. The concept of burnout/moral injury/disillusionment compounds this problem. There is evidence that shows that an increase in burnout leads to an increase in medical costs and also lowers patient safety. With this in mind, some of the things that attempt to mitigate rising medical costs with more administrative oversight and more healthcare policies might only increase costs. The potential of burnout at the same time makes it harder to create change. We believe what we have is a vicious cycle with burnout needing to be addressed at the same time as some of these other items are mitigated. Policies that increase administrative burdens without a direct value for patient care should be minimized. A lot of the challenging policies that managed care have implemented, including things like prior authorization, precertifications, denials of payment, and others, potentially increase frustration with the administrative aspects of medicine.

Healthcare Policies and Compliance

Privileging, Credentialing, Licensing, and Specialty Boards (ABIM)

In the absence of a national process inclusive of reporting and accountability, it is currently commonplace for providers with difficulties to move about the country. This poses a societal challenge in which the public is only as safe as their local state database allows. In addition, having this state-centric model creates challenges and inefficiencies for the providers themselves.

The quagmire that is embedded in healthcare credentialing/privileging is daunting. Every state has different rules and regulations for licensing, and every hospital does its own credentialing and privileging. In an era where telehealth and national healthcare delivery are becoming more prominent, work-arounds for licensing are really not enough. There needs to be centralization with common applications for licensing and hospital privileging. How much time and energy are spent filling out the same forms with the same information for every doctor? While there has been some local centralization of hospitals, there is no consistent process.

Each managed-care company also has its own application and process for becoming part of the payer plan. Physicians must be in multiple plans to survive. This requires applying to each of the payers and updating applications every few years. This is not a very good use of resources since the information is fundamentally the same.

We don't want to get into the controversy of licensing boards nor the controversies around physician maintenance of certification (MOC), but clearly this is another area where physicians are very frustrated with the time, complexity, and cost of maintaining specialty boards. There is much controversy as to whether this really contributes to quality. We will not come down on one side or another of the controversy, but only say that there has to be some resolution with the administrative and cost burden.

There are also many opportunities at the state level. These include modifying Medicaid payer models, utilizing Medicaid as an aggregator fostering alignment of metrics. They should enhance their role as policymakers to seek a balance between licensing flexibility and efficiency. They can and should provide technical assistance to providers.[10]

The Electronic Medical Record (EMR)

We have previously discussed the challenges and burdens created by the electronic medical record. According to author, celebrity, and practicing physician Atul Gawande, the electronic health record, which was "a system that promised to increase physician's mastery over the work has, instead, increased the work's mastery over them."[1] Multiple challenges exist including the proprietary nature of the systems, each requiring its own training and expertise. "Click fatigue" workflows are not intuitive for clinicians and of course the lack of true and complete interoperability. This latter issue will require reform of the certification requirements by the federal government, as well as a commitment to interoperability that will have to be driven by new policies. It will be necessary to require all vendors to use application programming interfaces (APIs) which allow patient data to be shared across competing technology platforms in the name of better care.

EMRs' documentation requirements for both government and private payers have dramatically increased. These requirements were developed many years ago and have not been updated. The EMRs could be dramatically improved to better communicate patient issues across all treating physicians and healthcare workers. Documentation guidelines were originally drafted with paper records in mind, and they need to be updated to reflect the EMR era. Changes should be made to the outdated Evaluation and Management (E/M) documentation guidelines and the ability to enter information from the care team should be explored. The primary purpose of the medical record should be patient care, not reimbursement.[11] The EMR should shift to a tool to care for the patient, not focused on billing or insurance or even data capture. While all the latter functions will need to be embedded, the primary function should be improving, documenting, and communicating care in the most efficient manner possible.

As a go-forward solution to these challenges, we believe we will have to dramatically increase physician engagement with design, implementation, and customization of EMRs. There will have to be a national commitment to resolving these interface or interoperability issues with specific efforts around legal and national policy changes to increase the user experience. To improve burnout, it is imperative that the EMR be easily usable.[1]

Only with the support of our communities and the public at large will legislative changes be established that require true interoperability and data transparency that reduce provider work burdens rather than increase them.

Telehealth

Telehealth and televisits are becoming more important to society as an access to care alternative. This use of telecommunications technology is a cost-effective and efficient model of delivering healthcare in the right situations. As telehealth becomes more mainstream and the time demands must be worked into a busy practice schedule, now is the opportunity to set proper policies, rules, and regulations across the states. Now is the chance to make this an efficient and effective model, unencumbered by intrastate complexities. We need to have some national policies that support these initiatives in a proactive fashion, both allowing it to occur and to do so with patient safety in mind. Physicians need to be involved in these discussions to best develop usable, patient-centric systems.

The Insurance Industry, Managed Care, All Those Authorizations

The American Academy of Family Physicians developed a prioritized list of principles for administrative simplification. Many of these are centered on managed care. These include a much more streamlined administrative version of many of the cumbersome office tasks, for example:

Prior authorizations: "These must be justified in terms of financial recovery, cost of administration, workflow burden, and lack of other feasible methods."[11]

Quality metrics: Provider and provider organizations are measuring quality and we believe this is the right thing to do for the sake of excellent patient care. The challenge is that everybody's measuring different metrics, and even when they measure the same metrics, they often have different criteria for numerators and denominators. This makes it almost impossible for the healthcare delivery system to keep track of all the different metrics and focus on them all in a logical fashion aimed at improved care outcomes across the industry. Often some of these metrics are more focused on process than on outcomes. On average, physicians submit these metrics to well over ten different provider organizations.[11] Quality metrics should focus on outcomes, not process, when practical and should be jointly agreed upon by the payer industry, the government, and the provider. There needs to be a consistent set of meaningful metrics. All reports should be simplified and unified so that physicians are not getting ten different utilization and quality reports from different sources that are often conflicting, confusing, and difficult to understand.

Formularies and other coverage issues: There is also an opportunity to become more consistent with formulary coverage and criteria for coverage. I understand the competitive advantages of having different formularies; however, can you imagine trying to manage that at either the provider or patient level. Some criteria with consistency on coverage criteria and formularies would go a long way toward simplifying a physician's practice.

Certification and documentation: Physicians want to order what the patient needs to maintain their health. The current procedure surrounding coverage of medical supplies, services, and other items contribute significantly to impeding efficient delivery of healthcare. Physicians' orders should be sufficient, and the physician should not have to sign multiple forms justifying durable medical equipment (DME), diabetic supplies, and other authorizations should be consistent and standardized.[11]

The Malpractice Crises, Not Forgotten

It is already been clearly documented that malpractice contributes to burnout, but also how burnout contributes to malpractice.[12, 13] The public outcry has gotten quieter in the last couple of years, but it is still very much part of every physician's day. A national solution would be an important additional factor in mitigating burnout. There are also significant cost implications.

More Physician Leadership. The Risk of Burnout in Physician Training Programs

One of the great challenges of burnout is that it can create its own burnout culture. This is particularly true in an academic and teaching environment. The image of future physicians is negatively affected if their instructor physicians are burned out. Students who work with burned-out physicians are more likely to burn out themselves. This, in turn, leads to future doctors who are already burned out or predisposed to burn out early in their student days. It was reported that students who experienced burnout are more likely to conduct themselves inappropriately.[14]

Engaged physician leadership is valuable for both mitigating burnout and improving engagement. This leadership comes to play as the characteristics of a physician's immediate supervisor links directly to burnout. Each one-point increase (on a five-point scale) in the leadership score of a physician's immediate supervisor decreases the odds of burnout by 3.3% and increases the likelihood of satisfaction by 9%.[15]

All That Wasted Time

There just is not enough time to do all the things that physicians need to do. The problem is that so much of that work is not really directed at patient care, and even if they only did patient care, it would still not be enough. As an example, a Duke University study estimated that if primary care physicians fulfill all of the recommended preventive care for the panel of 2,500 patients, they would need to work 21.7 hours a day.[16]

We must look at all the things that physicians and healthcare workers do that do not add value to patient care. We discussed a lot of those in prior chapters. One interesting effort has been called "trading time." In this situation, clinical time is traded for nonclinical time such as committees and volunteering that help the organization. This includes helping physicians directly with support services at home. A pilot program at Stanford allowed physicians to trade in time spent on committees with in-home services for themselves, such as cleaning and meal delivery. This has been shown to help burnout by integrating work and life challenges.[17]

When looking at administrative tasks, it is important to evaluate the time it takes to implement and operationalize the tasks and any possible return on investment. The human costs also need to be evaluated. There must be transparency and the cost and value of each task, or intervention, should be decided upon collaboratively rather than unilaterally. Essentially, this is simply the real-world application of the age-old golden rule: Treat people the way you wish to be treated. None of us want to have our workflows changed without our input. Hence, while a more systematic approach is essential, it needs to be undertaken with the full participation of the people closest to the processes.[18]

Physician Shortage

The US Department of Health and Human Services (HHS) has predicted a shortage of up to 90,000 physicians by the year 2025. One of the underlying drivers of this shortage will be the loss of physicians from burnout. One estimate of the lost revenue per full-time equivalent physician is $990,000.[1] There has always been, and continues to be, a geographic misalignment of physicians as well. If we think about all of the potential fallout from burnout, the risk of physician shortages becomes even more acute. If one includes physicians retiring early or cutting back on their hours or even becoming less efficient with their current hours, the risk of not having physicians available is very real. Each one-point increase in burnout (on a seven-point scale) is associated with a 30 to 40% increase in the likelihood that that physician will reduce the work hours in the next two years. Burnout is estimated to contribute to a 1% reduction in physician work effort, which equates to losing the graduates of seven medical schools annually.[19]

It is also important to mention that many physicians are leaving clinical practice for nonclinical jobs. Other physicians are moving into a concierge practice and limiting their patient populations. Both of these are added challenges to physician shortages.

Nursing shortages are also very real. Over the years, many of the more experienced nurses have left the acute care setting. If the issues of nursing and healthcare worker burnout continue, this could drive the price of healthcare up even further, creating a vicious cycle.

Other aspects of nursing shortages get down to the challenge of a burnout culture at either the hospital or the outpatient facility. Burnout is a cultural issue and can lead to a shortage of physicians and all hospital personnel or outpatient personnel in this chaotic and frustrating environment.

Advanced Practice Providers (nurse practitioners and physician assistants) have the additional frustration of needing clarification on a national level of where they fit into the delivery system. States can help by developing appropriate and consistent licensing.

Dealing with the Stigma of Mental Health in Physicians and Healthcare Workers

We must provide easy access to mental health services for physicians and healthcare workers. From a policy standpoint, there must be a "safe haven." There needs to be a way to not report applicants for licensure who are receiving appropriate treatment for mental health and substance abuse issues.[1] There must be an element of privacy and a fair and equitable way to deal with this for licensing, managed-care contracting, and hospital privileging. There is an opportunity for statewide physician health programs (PHPs) to act as advocates for physicians and deal with these mental health issues. In 2018, the Federation of State Medical Boards adopted a policy recommended in 2016 that called for reconsidering probing questions about physician mental health, addiction, or substance abuse on applications for medical licensure or renewal.[1]

We must look at mental health issues in an entirely new way. Over 50% of physicians have symptoms of burnout, and many of those have depression and challenges with substance abuse. Figure 11.2

The Volume-to-Value Transition

The transition from volume to value is critical in removing some of the misaligned incentives in day-to-day practice. In a more perfect world, physicians would be compensated for the right care instead of doing more care. An example of this might be calling patients or telehealth rather than insisting on office visits. Presumably physicians would have smaller panels, have more time to spend with patients, and be encouraged to use team-based care models. These models will reward outcomes. The other part of these models is that they put the delivery system with physicians and other healthcare workers

Drivers of burnout and engagement in physicians	Individual factors	Work unit factors	Organization factors	National factors
Workload and job demands	• Specialty • Practice location • Decision to increase work to increase income	• Productivity expectations • Team structure • Efficiency • Use of allied health professionals	• Productivity targets • Method of compensation - Salary - Productivity based • Payer mix	• Structure reimbursement - Medicare/Medicaid - Bundled payments - Documentation requirements
Efficiency and resources	• Experience • Ability to prioritize • Personal efficiency • Organizational skills • Willingness to delegate • Ability to say "no"	• Availability of support staff and their experience • Patient check-in efficiency/process • Use of scribes • Team huddles • Use of allied health professionals	• Integration of care • Use of patient portal • Institutional efficiency: - EHR - Appointment system - Ordering systems • How regulations interpreted and applied	• Integration of care • Requirements for: - Electronic prescribing - Medication reconciliation - Meaningful use of EHR • Certification agency facility regulations (JCAHO) • Precertifications for tests/treatments
Meaning in work	• Self-awareness of most personally meaningful aspect of work • Ability to shape career to focus on interests • Doctor–patient relationships • Personal recognition of positive events at work	• Match of work to talents and interests of individuals • Opportunities for involvement - Education - Research - Leadership	• Organizational culture • Practice environment • Opportunities for professional development	• Evolving supervisory role of physicians (potentially less direct patient contact) • Reduced funding - Research - Education • Regulations that increase clerical work
Culture and values	• Personal values • Professional values • Level of altruism • Moral compass/ethics • Commitment to organization	• Behavior of work unit leader • Work unit norms and expectations • Equity/fairness	• Organization's mission - Service/quality vs profit • Organization's values • Behavior of senior leaders • Communication/ messaging • Organizational norms and expectations • Just culture	• System of coverage for uninsured • Structure reimbursement - What is rewarded • Regulations
Control and flexibility	• Personality • Assertiveness • Intentionality	• Degree of flexibility: - Control of physician calendars - Clinic start/end times - Vacation scheduling - Call schedule	• Scheduling system • Policies • Affiliations that restrict referrals • Rigid application practice guidelines	• Precertifications for tests/ treatments • Insurance networks that restrict referrals • Practice guidelines
Social support and community at work	• Personality traits • Length of service • Relationship-building skills	• Collegiality in practice environment • Physical configuration of work unit space • Social gatherings to promote community • Team structure	• Collegiality across the organization • Physician lounge • Strategies to build community • Social gatherings	• Support and community created by Medical/specialty societies
Work-life integration	• Priorities and values • Personal characteristics - Spouse/partner - Children/dependents - Health issues	• Call schedule • Structure night/weekend coverage • Cross-coverage for time away • Expectations/role models	• Vacation policies • Sick/medical leave • Policies - Part-time work - Flexible scheduling • Expectations/role models	• Requirements for: - Maintenance certification - Licensing • Regulations that increase clerical work

FIGURE 3. Drivers of burnout and engagement with examples of individual, work unit, organization, and national factors that influence each driver. EHR = electronic health record; JCAHO = Joint Commission on the Accreditation of Healthcare Organizations. Adapted from *Mayo Clin Proc.*[39]

Figure 11.2 Drivers of burnout and engagement. Reprinted from *Mayo Clinic Proceedings*: 92 (1): Tate Shanafelt MD and John Noseworthy MD, CEO: Executive leadership and physician well-being: nine organizational strategies to promote engagement and reduce burnout, pages 129–146, copyright January 2017, with permission from Elsevier.

back in charge of what they do and how they do it. Many believe this model would help mitigate burnout and bring back some of the joy in practicing medicine.

One of the challenges for many healthcare and provider systems is the transition period in moving from fee-for-service to value-based contracting. Having multiple and mixed payment models with differing performance metrics and differing incentives contributes to a sense of chaos thus contributing to frustrations and burnout.

It Is Time to Start a National Conversation

It is time to bring this issue to the forefront of a national conversation. A recent article discussed the importance of leaderships getting involved and identified ten large healthcare system CEOs who have committed to engaging on this issue. They committed to 11 different actions[6]:

1. Readily measure the well-being of physicians at their institutions using a standardized instrument
2. Include measures of physician well-being on their institutional performance dashboards
3. Track institutional cost of physician turnover, early retirement, and reductions in clinical effort
4. Emphasize the importance of leadership skill development for physicians and their managers
5. Address the clerical burden and inappropriate allocation of work to physicians
6. Support team-based models of care
7. Encourage government regulators to address the burden of unnecessary and redundant regulations
8. Support the AMA and other national organizations
9. Share anti-burnout best practices
10. Educate CEOs and other stakeholders about the importance of reducing burnout

11. Conduct research to determine the most effective policy interventions to improve the well-being of the healthcare workforce

Summary

As we can see from the above narratives, burnout is not simply an individual problem. It is deep rooted in the healthcare system and has the potential to affect those who work in healthcare as well as those who need healthcare. The solutions, therefore, must be broader than the local interventions with true political and grassroots support.

Bibliography

1. Jha, A.K., Ilif, A.R. & Chaoui, A.A. A crisis in healthcare: A call to action on physician burnout, Harvard global health Institute. Retrieved from http://www.massmed.org/news-and-publications/mms-news-releases/physician-burnout-report-2018/.
2. Chan, T.H. (2019, January) Leading healthcare organizations to clear position burnout as “public health crises”, Harvard school of public health. Retrieved from https://www.hsph.harvard.edu/news/press-releases/leading-health-care-organizations-declare-physician-burnout-as-public-health-crisis/
3. McHugh, Matthew D., Kutney-Lee, A., Cimiotti, J.P., et al. (2011). Nurses widespread job satisfaction, burnout, and frustration with patients' health benefits signal problems for patient care. *Health Affairs* (project code), *30*(2), 202–210, PMC.
4. Pfeiffer, Rebecca (2019, May 28). Physician Burnout cost industry 4.6 billion Annually, Healthcare Dive. Retrieved from https://www.healthcaredive.com/news/physician-burnout-costs-industry-46b-annually/555631/.
5. National academy of medicine: Action collaborative on clinical well-being and resilience. Retrieved from https://nam.edu/action-collaborative-on-clinician-well-being-and-resilience-network-organizations/.

6. Butcher, Lola (2017, September 22). Starting a national conversation about burnout: AHA speakers bureau. Retrieved from https://www.hhnmag.com/articles/8608-starting-a-national-conversation-about-burnout.
7. Steps forward, AMA. Retrieved from https://edhub.ama-assn.org/steps-forward.
8. Henry, A.T. (2017, May 10). Burnout: Six boosters for research to improve physician well-being, physician health, AMA. Retrieved from https://www.ama-assn.org/practice-management/physician-health/burnout-6-boosters-research-improve-physician-well-being.
9. Feeley, Derek (2017, November 28). The triple aim or the quadruple aim? Four points to help set your strategy. Retrieved from http://www.ihi.org/communities/blogs/the-triple-aim-or-the-quadruple-aim-four-points-to-help-set-your-strategy.
10. Reck, J. (2017, January 9). *Primary care Provider Burnout: Implications for States & Strategies for Mitigation*. Retrieved from https://nashp.org/primary-care-provider-burnout-implications-for-states-strategies-for-mitigation/.
11. Principles for administrative simplification. Retrieved from https://www.aafp.org/about/policies/all/principles-adminsimplification.html.
12. Kopynec, Suze. (2019, May 1). Provider burnout and the risk of malpractice. *APA News*. Retrieved from https://www.aapa.org/news-central/2018/05/provider-burnout-and-the-risk-of-malpractice/.
13. Becker's Hospital News. (2011, November 15). *Malpractice Lawsuits Linked to Physician Burnout, Dissatisfaction*. Retrieved from https://www.beckershospitalreview.com/news-analysis/malpractice-lawsuits-linked-to-physician-burnout-dissatisfaction.html.
14. Hamlin, A. (2016, August 1). *Physician Burnout: What it is and its Impact on Future Doctors*. Retrieved from https://www.studentdoctor.net/2016/08/01/physician-burnout-impact-future-doctors/.
15. Noseworthy, J., Madara, J., Cosgrove, D., et al. (2017, March 28). *Physician Burnout is a Public Health Crisis: A Message to Our Fellow Health Care CEO's*. Retrieved from https://www.healthaffairs.org/do/10.1377/hblog20170328.059397/full/.
16. Altschuler, Justin, Margolius, David, Grumbach, K. (2012, September/October). Estimating reasonable panel size for primary care. *The Annals of Family Medicine, 10*(5), 396–4000. http://www.annfammed.org/content/10/5/396.full.

17. Silcott, Sasha. (2018, July 31). Clinician burnout: Be part of the solution, med page today's Kevin M.D. Retrieved from https://www.kevinmd.com/blog/2018/07/clinician-burnout-be-part-of-the-solution.html.
18. Erickson, S.M., Rockwern, B., Koltov, M., & McLean, R.M. (2017, May 2). Putting patients first by reducing administrative tasks in health care: A position paper of the American College of Physicians. *Annals of Internal Medicine, 166*(9), 659–661.
19. Shanafeld, T.D., Mungo, M., Schmitgen, J. et al. (2016). A longitudinal study evaluating the association between physician burnout and changes in professional work effort. *Mayo Clinic Proceedings, 91*(4), 422–431.
20. Burnett, J. (2019, January 31). Here's *Why* Physician Burnout Is Officially "A Public Health Crisis". Retrieved from https://thriveglobal.com/stories/physician-burnout-public-health-crisis-solutions-report/.
21. Dyrbye, L.N., & Shanafelt, T.D. (2011). Physician burnout: A potential threat to successful health care reform. *JAMA, 305*(19), 2009–2010.
22. Farley, H. *Strategies for Achieving Joy in the Workplace.* PowerPoint Presentation.
23. Jha, A.K., Iliff, A.R., Chaoui, A.A., et al. (2019, March 28). *A Crisis in Health Care: A Call to Action on Physician Burnout.* Retrieved from http://www.massmed.org/News-and-Publications/MMS-News-Releases/A-Crisis-in-Health-Care--A-Call-to-Action-on--Physician-Burnout/#.XWc3vehKjIU.
24. Joy, J. (2017, April 11). *A Broader View of Solutions for the Physician Burnout Public Health Crisis: Prevention and Recovery.* Retrieved from https://www.beckershospitalreview.com/hospital-physician-relationships/a-broader-view-of-solutions-for-the-physician-burnout-public-health-crisis-prevention-and-recovery.html.
25. Montgomery, A. (2014). The inevitability of physician burnout: Implications for interventions. *Sciencedirect, 1*(1), 50–56.
26. Nash, D. (2018, February 16). *Physician Burnout: What Can Be Done?* Retrieved from https://www.medpagetoday.com/publichealthpolicy/generalprofessionalissues/71204.
27. Ochoa, P. (2018). Impact of burnout on organizational outcomes, the influence of legal demands: The case of Ecuadorian physicians. *Frontiers in Psychology, 9*, 662.

28. Perlo, J., Balik, B., Swensen, S., et al. (2017). *IHI Framework for Improving Joy in Work*. IHI White Paper. Cambridge, MA: Institute for Healthcare Improvement.
29. Shin, A., Gandhi, T., Herzig, S. (2016, April 21). *Make the Clinician Burnout Epidemic a National Priority*. Retrieved from https://www.healthaffairs.org/do/10.1377/hblog20160421.054511/full/
30. *Top 10 Culture Change Interventions to Reduce Burnout and Improve Physician Well-Being*. American College of Physicians. Retrieved from https://www.acponline.org/practice-resources/physician-well-being-and-professional-satisfaction/top-10-culture-change-interventions-to-reduce-burnout-and-improve-physician-well-being.

Chapter 12

Moving Past Burnout to Engagement and Joy

George Mayzell

Contents

We have spent a lot of time talking about burnout and its challenges, opportunities, and impact on the delivery of healthcare. One hopes that in the next few years we can slowly mitigate some of the things that are causing burnout. It is very clear that it will take a lot longer to truly eliminate some of the global items.

Although it is not a linear or direct connection, it would be nice to see a movement from burnout to "joy" in medicine. Currently most physicians are not recommending that their children go into medicine.[1] It would be very nice to see that change. It would also be nice to see the satisfaction and the patient gratitude that were once part of delivering medical care return to the profession. While this may seem a little idealistic, it is not out of reach.

Somewhere between burnout and joy is the reality of physician and healthcare worker engagement. It is hard to know exactly where on the scale engagement fits; however, if physicians or healthcare workers are engaged, this goes a long way toward mitigating or even eliminating burnout. It is really not the opposite of burnout but more of a part of the nonlinear journey from burnout to engagement (and joy). While burnout and joy are not mutually exclusive, they do complement each other.

When organizations have engaged employees, the bottom line is higher, their turnover is lower, and they are more likely to develop, attract, and retain high-caliber employees.[2] It is therefore a competitive advantage to have engaged employees.

A definition of engagement is the "active and positive contribution of doctors within their normal working roles to maintaining and enhancing the performance of the organization."[2, 3] Another definition of engagement is "a workforce that holds a positive attitude toward the organization and its values, and is foundational to creating high-performing organizations."[4]

There are many contributors to engagement, which include having confidence and trust in the organization. Physicians and healthcare workers must believe that the organization cares about quality and believe that it treats physicians and staff with respect. Figure 12.1 displays a list of these qualities.[2]

There is a multitude of studies that show that improving engagement contributes to improved performance, professional productivity, and lower turnover rates, while joy improves patient experience, outcomes, and safety, and leads to lower costs.[6, 7]

This level of engagement and trust can be measured by the Medical Engagement Scale (MES) that was recently developed

Drivers for Physician Engagement

- Willing to recommend your organization to friends and family
- Believing the organization cares about its customers
- Physicians and executives goals are aligned
- The organization provides excellent care and service to patients
- The organization treats physicians and staff with respect
- Physicians and staff have reasonable autonomy
- The organization supports work life balance
- The organization listens to physician and staff input
- There is teamwork at the organization
- The organization supports professional development
- The organization supports physician and nursing leadership

Figure 12.1 Drivers for physician engagement. Based on Hudec, B (June 2015). The 12 statements that define your physicians' engagement. Advisory Board, retrieved from https://www.advisory.com/research/medical-group-strategy-council/practice-notes/2015/june/who-is-to-blame-for-physician-burnout and Kaissi, A. (2012). A Road Map for Trust: Enhancing Physician Engagement. Regina Qu'Appelle Health Region. Retrieved fromhttps://pdfs.semanticscholar.org/b9a1/9f415e24b3462537499d7a11c3b0c0226bb9.pdf.

in the UK. This includes measurements of feeling valued, feeling empowered, having purpose and direction, and working in an open culture.

The Institute for Healthcare Improvement (IHI) has recommended a framework for engaging physicians in quality and safety that stresses a common purpose. It focuses on developing a compact between physicians and the institution, and a framework that includes:

- Developing clear and efficient communication channels with physicians
- Building trust, understanding, and respect
- Identifying and developing physician leaders

Action steps that are suggested are to (1) hold formal and informal face-to-face meetings with physicians and listen to

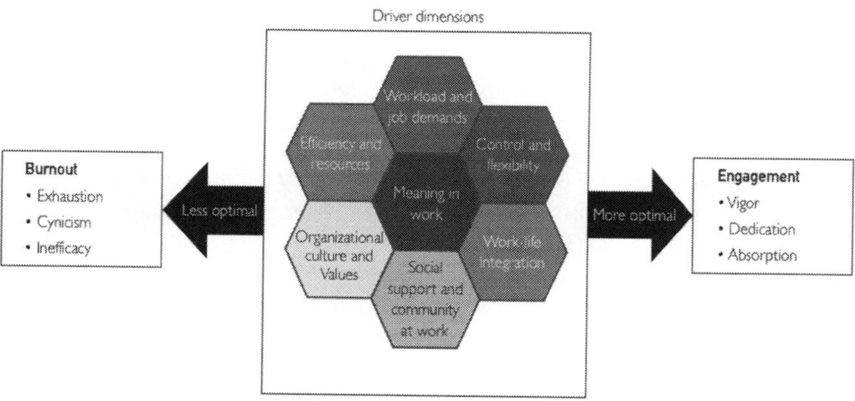

Figure 12.2 Drivers of burnout and engagement. Reprinted from *Mayo Clinic Proceedings*: 92 (1): Tate Shanafelt, MD, and John Noseworthy, MD, CEO: Executive Leadership and Physician Well-being: Nine Organizational Strategies to Promote Engagement and Eeduce Burnout, pages 129–146 copyright January 2017, with permission from Elsevier.[8]

their issues, (2) involve physicians in the majority of managerial decisions and strategic plans (3) and create formal training and development opportunities for physicians to refine their leadership skills.[2]

In Figure 12.2 from Mayo Clinic, there is a focus on physician well-being. The driver dimensions and linkages that help to move you through the nonlinear continuum of burnout to engagement are displayed.

Moving from Engagement to Physician Well-Being

As we shift gears from simply mitigating burnout and encouraging engagement, we are moving toward the concept of physician well-being and bringing back some of the joy that should be part of healthcare delivery. This movement is a shared responsibility for the professionals involved, their employers, and society.

Shanafelt et al. suggest that there are nine strategies to promote engagement, reduce burnout, and promote physician well-being. These include:[8]

- Acknowledge and assess the problem
- Harness leadership
- Develop targeted interventions
- Cultivate community at work
- Use rewards and incentives wisely
- Align and strengthen culture
- Promote flexibility and work/ life integration
- Provide resources to promote resilience and self-care and
- Facilitate and fund organizational science

This list of strategies, if one looks carefully, represents good healthcare business strategies for any healthcare organization.

Using these strategies, Mayo Clinic had their absolute burnout rate of physicians decrease by 7% despite an 11% rise in burnout of physicians nationally using identical metrics.[8, 9] They also were able to reduce the rate of burnout in non-physician employees. They still acknowledge that there is a long way to go.

Creating a Framework and Process to Bring Back the Joy in Medicine

According to Don Berwick, "joy in work" is not flaky. Improving joy in work is possible, important, and effective in pursuit of the triple aim.[10]

The AMA through their STEPS Forward program suggests nine steps to create the organizational foundation to help move toward joy in medicine. They suggest a total of nine steps. These include:

- Creating a Culture of Wellness (check list)
- Engage senior leadership
- Track the business case for well-being

- Resource wellness infrastructure
- Measure wellness
- Strengthen local leadership
- Develop and evaluate interventions
- Efficiency of practice
  - Improve workflow efficiency and maximize the power of team-based care
  - Reduce clerical burden and tame the EHR
- Enhance personal resilience
  - Support the physical and psychosocial health of the workforce

AMA STEPS Forward, Rating an Organization's Foundation for Joy in Medicine[11]

One of the key issues here is to create a culture of wellness. Using the list above, these separate projects and processes must become integrated into the day-to-day operations of an organization. These items may or may not work individually, but as a group they can create a change in culture that allows the organization to move past burnout into engagement and perhaps toward "joy." Creating this new culture must be an organizational imperative. It will have to start with leadership and permeate through the entire organization.

According to IHI, moving to joy begins by asking questions that drive to the heart of the workplace culture. These include:

- What makes for a good day for you?
- What makes you proud to work here?
- When we are at our best, what does it look like?

Everyone must feel like their ideas are heard. There must be a commitment to a systems approach with a shared responsibility at all levels of the organization to create this new culture. It includes huddles, workshops, and open communication. It includes physical safety and also psychological safety. Psychological safety is founded on respect among all stakeholders and rapid interventions for any disrespectful behavior.[10] This includes any time of bullying behavior.

Simple things include pushing decision-making down to the staff level. Autonomy is critical. Staff need to be engaged in decision-making. There should be camaraderie and teamwork with appropriate rewards and recognition. There also needs to be a focus on continuous improvement processes at the cultural level and, of course, real-time measurements. In fact, wellness/culture/joy metrics should be part of the CEO- and board-level tracking dashboards.

How to Measure Joy in the Workplace

There are several tools to help measure wellness and joy in the workplace. These are very different tools from those used to measure burnout. As we move from burnout to wellness, it is important to start measuring not just the absence of the negative. We need to also measure positive behaviors such as engagement, wellness, and joy. These tools include things such as:

Mayo Well-Being Index[12]

Mayo Clinic offers all of its employees access to wellness assessment. This allows individuals to calibrate their well-being relative to that of their peers. It is anonymous, and individual scoring is private with the aggregate score being evaluated by the system. It is a nine-question survey that has been well validated.

Net Promoter Scores[13]

The Net promoter Score (NPS) was originally devised by the *Harvard Business Review* to indicate customer engagement.

Individuals are asked how likely they are to recommend this company as a place to work. The ratios are then calculated on the number promoters minus the number detractors divided by the total number of respondents. This may be a good metric to evaluate an organization. There are also more complicated versions of net promoter scores that have additional metrics as part of the calculation.[10]

Mayo Clinic Leadership Dimension Assessment[10, 14]

Leadership is recognized as being closely associated with burnout and engagement. Surveys looking at the relationship between supervisor leadership note that there is a strong correlation between burnout and leadership. IHI has created a short assessment tool, which is adapted from the Mayo Clinic assessment model. The IHI tool highlights the most important dimensions of leadership.[10]

There are several other measurement tools that measure physician engagement, patient safety, and other important characteristics. As we discussed in detail in Chapter 5, there is also a number of tools that focus more directly on measuring burnout and depression.

Creating a Culture of Wellness and Joy

So, how do we create a culture of wellness and joy? This is about moving past burnout and creating satisfaction in the workplace. The Standford wellness model uses a survey which includes questions that focus on[15;]

- Perceived appreciation
- Personal/organization values alignment
- Peer supportiveness
- Perceived support from leadership
- Control of schedule

It is important that organizations and physicians start to focus on helping and working with each other. This includes healing the healer concepts, physician mentorships, and wellness champions. They must focus on success and communication. There needs to be a psychological safety zone for physicians to share stories with each other and understand that they are not alone. Sharing stories helps them reconnect with what originally brought them to medicine.[16]

We must heal the professional culture of medicine. We must acknowledge the complexity of healthcare delivery and understand how difficult it is to practice healthcare in today's complex environment.[17] An interesting concept of "the manageable cockpit" for clinicians notes that in other industries we have taken the time to understand the human implications of information flow and the impact of work on an environment, but not for physicians. If we think of piloting an airplane, there have been many studying on helping the pilot prioritize and manage the large amount of information inputs. The amount of information and complexity needs to be simplified and codified, understanding that a human being must be able to react and thrive in the healthcare environment. Experts suggest:

- We develop and measure a manageable cockpit that captures cognitive workload.
- We establish clinician well-being as a health system metric.
- We encourage and apply research regarding interventions to create a more manageable cockpit.
- We establish best practices to support these endeavors.

We must hold all stakeholders, including institution, payers, technology vendors, state and federal agencies, and developers of clinical metrics accountable for supporting these endeavors.[18]

There is also the SELF CARE model which has been developed by the Hawaii Permanente Medical Group (HPMG). This model has several components that are part of the title. SELF CARE is an acronym that stands for sleep, exercise, love and laughter, food, compassion, awe, resilience, and engagement. These eight components focus on different aspects of care delivery. The first four focus on the individual and the last four focus on the process of engagement.

Another model from the Atlanta Permanente Medical Group is called JAMM, which stands for "joy and meaning in medicine." The JAMM model is focused on "exceptional care experience"; this is for both the patient and the care teams. All agree that leadership both at the physician level and at the organizational level are critical in implementing these culture-changing programs.[19]

Stanford also has a program focused on wellness and physician joy. It is called Stanford Medicine's WellMD. The Stanford model focuses on a culture of wellness, efficiency of practice, and personal resilience. All these things help to keep the focus on professional fulfillment. WellMD acknowledges that a lot of the challenge of a practicing physician is practice efficiency. They need to look through the eyes of the physician to make sure the appropriate priorities are considered[20] (Figure 12.3).

Summary

We must try to bring back the patient-physician relationships into healthcare. These relationships need to extend from the physician to the patient, but also include physician professionalism. It is important that we reconnect the physician and other healthcare workers to the purpose of healing and allow them to focus on what they do best in a comprehensible, manageable, and meaningful engagement. We need to encourage trust between physicians and patients as well as

Figure 12.3 Professional wellness and cultural model. Shanafelt, T, Swenson, SJ, Woody, J, Levin, J, Lille, J, Physician and Nurse Well-Being. Seven Things Hospital Boards Should Know. *J Healthcare Mgmt*. 2018; 63:363–369 Copyright (©) 2016 The Board of trustees of the Leland Stanford Junior University. All rights reserved.

among those in the healthcare industry. There needs to be continuous learning and a commitment to doing research to look at integration of all the factors that go into delivering good healthcare. We must commit to more research to make and keep our medical delivery system the best in the world. We have one of the best healthcare systems, but we will need to work to keep it that way. We must invest in keeping the staff healthy and engaged and committed to patients and patient care.

Bibliography

1. Lagresse, Jeff. (2018, October 1). Why 70% of physicians would not recommend the profession. Retrieved from https://www.healthcarefinancenews.com/news/why-70-percent-physicians-would-not-recommend-profession.
2. Kaissi, A. (2012). A road map for trust: Enhancing physician engagement. *Regina Qu'Appelle Health Region*. Retrieved from https://pdfs.semanticscholar.org/b9a1/9f415e24b3462537499d7a11c3b0c0226bb9.pdf.
3. Spureon, P., Mazelan, P.M., & Barwell, F. (2011). Medical engagement: A crucial underpinning to organizational performance. *Health Services Management Research, 24*(3), 114–120.
4. Robinson, D., Perryman, S., & Hayday, S. (2004). *The Drivers of Employee Engagement.* Brighton, UK: Institute for Employment Studies. Retrieved from https://www.employment-studies.co.uk/system/files/resources/files/408.pdf.
5. Hudec, B. (2015, June). The 12 statements that define your physician engagement. advisory board. Retrieved from https://www.advisory.com/research/medical-group-strategy-council/practice-notes/2015/june/who-is-to-blame-for-physician-burnout.
6. Harter, J.K., Schmidt, F.L., & Hayes, T.L. (2002). Business unit level relationship between employee satisfaction, employee engagement, and business outcomes: A meta-analysis. *The Journal of Applied Psychology, 87*(2), 268–279.
7. Burton, J. (2008). The business case for healthy workplace. *Industrial Accident Prevention Association*. Retrieved from https://www.uml.edu/docs/fd_business_case_healthy_workplace_tcm18-42671.pdf.
8. Shanafelt, T.D., & Noseworthy, J.H. (2017). Executive leadership and physician well-being: Nine organizational strategies to promote engagement and reduce burnout. *Mayo Clinic Proceedings, 92*(1), 129–146.
9. Shanafelt, T.D., Hasan, O., & Dyrbye, L.N. et al. (2015). Changes in burnout and satisfaction with work–life balance physicians and the general US working population between 2011 and 2014. *Mayo Clinic Proceedings, 90*(12), 1600–1613.
10. Perlo, J., Balik, B., Swensen, S., et al. (2017). *IHI Framework for Improving Joy in Work.* IHI white paper. Cambridge, MA: Institute for healthcare improvement. (available@ihi.org).

11. Steps forward, AMA. Retrieved from https://edhub.ama-assn.org/steps-forward.
12. Program on physician well-being, Mayo clinic research. Retrieved from https://www.mayo.edu/research/centers-programs/program-physician-well-being.
13. Reichheld, F.F. (2003, December). The one number you need to grow. *Harvard Business Review*. Retrieved from https://hbr.org/2003/12/the-one-number-you-need-to-grow.
14. Shanafelt, T.D., Gorringe, G., Menaker, R., et al. (2015). The impact of organizational leadership on physician burnout and satisfaction. *Mayo Clinic Proceedings, 90*(4), 432–440.
15. Lola, Butcher. (2017, September 21). Case study: Stanford medicine seeks to understand burnouts are measurement. Retrieved from https://www.hhnmag.com/articles/8585-case-study-stanford-medicine-seeks-to-understand-burnout-through-measurement.
16. Seto, B. (2018, August 13). The road to physician wellness: Permanente medical groups work to foster culture of wellness and improve physician resilience. Retrieved from https://permanente.org/road-physician-wellness/.
17. Shanafelt, T.D., Schein, E., Minor, L.B., et al. (2019). Healing the professional culture of medicine.
18. Sinsky, C.A., & Privitera, M.R. (2018). Creating a "manageable cockpit" for clinicians: A shared responsibility. *JAMA Internal Medicine, 178*(6), 741–742.
19. Seto, B. (2018, August 6). Caring for those who provide care, Permanente medicine. Retrieved from https://permanente.org/caring-provide-care/.
20. Murphy, M.L., de Vries, P., Trockel, M., et al. (2017). Stanford medicine. Retrieved from https://wellmd.stanford.edu/content/dam/sm/wellmd/documents/2017-wellmd-status-report-dist-1.pdf, Well Medcenter status report.
21. Erickson, S.M., Rockwern, B., Koltov, M., et al. (2017, May 2). *Putting Patient First by Reducing Administrative Tasks in Health Care: A Position Paper of the American College of Physicians*. Retrieved from https://annals.org/aim/fullarticle/2614079/putting-patients-first-reducing-administrative-tasks-health-care-position-paper
22. Nash, D. (2018, February 16). *Physician Burnout: What Can Be Done?* Retrieved from https://www.medpagetoday.com/publichealthpolicy/generalprofessionalissues/71204

23. Inha, P. (2017, September 18). *How to Find Joy in Practicing Medicine*. Retrieved from https://www.kevinmd.com/blog/2017/09/find-joy-practicing-medicine.html
24. Sinsky, C., Shanafelt, T., Murphy, M.L., et al. (2017, September 7). Creating the organizational foundation for joy in medicine. Retrieved from https://edhub.ama-assn.org/steps-forward/module/2702510.
25. Wright, A.A., & Katz, I.T. (2018). Beyond burnout – redesigning care to restore meaning and sanity for physicians. *The New England Journal of Medicine*, 378(4), 309–311.

Index